The Sky Begins
At Your Feet

*a memoir on cancer,
community, and coming
home to the body*

Caryn Mirriam-Goldberg

Ice Cube Books
North Liberty, Iowa

THE SKY BEGINS AT YOUR FEET
A memoir on cancer, community,
and coming home to the body

Copyright © 2009 Caryn Mirriam-Goldberg

ISBN 9781888160437

Second Printing

Library of Congress Control Number: 2008943267

Ice Cube Books & Press (est. 1993)
205 North Front Street
North Liberty, Iowa 52317-9302
fax 1.413.451.0223
www.icecubepress.com
steve@icecubepress.com

Printed in Canada

The paper used in this publication meets the minimum requirements
of the American National Standard for Information Sciences—
Permanence of Paper for Printed Library Materials, ANSI Z39.48-1992

Cover: *Prairie Sky—Autumn Wine* painting by Joan Foth used
by permission from Karen and John MacFarland. Special thanks
to Joan Foth for her art, Karen and John MacFarland for use of
the art, and photographer Jerry Sipe for photographing the art.

Praise for
The Sky Begins At Your Feet

A Midwest Connections Pick
by the Midwest Independent Booksellers Association

"If you're going to write about your breast cancer diagnosis,
it doesn't hurt being the poet laureate of Kansas. With a
poet's eye and lyricism, Mirriam-Goldberg describes all
the emotions and trials patients and their families
experience, allowing readers to see past the struggle to
the richness beyond. Highly recommended."
—*Library Journal*, starred review

"An amazing story worthy of the reader's
time and attention."
—*Oncolink*, Abramson Cancer Center
of the University of Pennsylvania

"I think a memoir such as this is like a little shining
light of hope for those going through cancer or those living
with others enduring it."
—*Peeking Between The Pages*

"Experience this lively story, which ends with brief accounts
of six anniversaries post treatment. Creativity, chemistry,
and body love have won."
—*The Iowa Source*

"Her book describes the process by which she learned to love
her body and to look at herself without judgment."
—*Publishers Weekly*

Table of Contents

I love this body that's not the way I thought.
I love these people who help me through the dark.
I love this life that keeps me waking up.

—Kelley Hunt & Caryn Mirriam-Goldberg,
from "Love Heals"

For my children,
Daniel, Natalie and Forest

Preface: Singing the Body Electric

I cannot figure out who I am as a body these days. I look in the mirror each morning, each night. I look right into the scars, trying to read them like the dreams I have at night of driving around lost for hours, or not being able to make a call on a pay phone without punching in the wrong numbers. There is always an emergency.

Right before the sleep that might take me back to such dreams, I touch my chest—feel the lines, and the numbness too, try to measure with my fingers where feeling begins and where the zone of only feeling the pressure of the touch is. Sometimes I use my husband's hand to show me where the nerve endings are and aren't anymore. Fortunately, his hands, and the rest of him, don't seem at all distracted by the absence of these parts of me. On very hot nights I lie under the swooshing ceiling fan naked, feeling a little like an extraterrestrial woman, shaped differently but generally looking the same as most women from a distance. The bed is large, a soft boat under the circular winds of the changing world.

I get up in the morning and always put my glasses on first, then strap on my fake breasts, which have spent the night hanging out in the nifty pockets of my special bra. There is little difference between the glasses and the boobs to me, just things I wear when I'm awake, each an item to bridge the world between my dreams and waking time, between whoever I am and the rest of the living world. Each is a prop, something that fills out space,

1

contributes to how I see or am seen, my prosthesis something between person and garment.

Each day I walk among the other bodies, lately not so concerned with glancing at women's breasts, the ones not cut away and replaced by impostors. I find myself immediately thinking, in some kind of reptile brain way, that their breasts must be fake, rebuilt, or real but soon to be taken away. I pause and remind myself that I'm simply projecting my thoughts, from the dark and dry place I usually can't reach in my mind, onto others. Sometimes I remember to remember that everyone has their own scars and numbness, most of these wounds not even physical.

Yet at the same time, I find myself often extremely confused about what it is to live in a woman's body without breasts. Of course, I know that breasts are just a body part, not a gender identity, but there's something about losing this part of me, this part I would hold gently on cold nights as I slept to keep them warm. This part round and lovely, traveling effortlessly with me, quiet mourning doves sleeping soundly on my chest. It's inconceivable that such a part could be gone, that I would have chosen to give it up, that there's so little evidence of their existence in my memory.

That's part of the problem: in my memory, below the surface of words and rational understanding, breasts are part of being erotic. The breasts are a playground of great sensation and lushness. Without them, what does it mean to make love? What does it mean to love my own body?

So I am trying to love my body for what it is right now. Let the love I feel for it—the tenderness for my moving fingers on the keyboard, the appreciation for the strength of my legs to carry me for miles on an early spring day, the wonder at the softness of my skin, the shapes I leave in the blankets. Let this love be enough.

Let this love show me the way to sing the body electric, to write the body erotic.

Let me learn this way of loving what's imperfect from the land and sky around me, the best mirror to show us that what we do to our environment, we also do to ourselves. As well, the earth where I live is the best teacher when it comes to persevering through the seasons with the kind of grace that celebrates life, however it comes—in the icy wind mid-winter that makes the windows tremble, the explosion of lilac one particularly slow spring, the reddening grasses late fall, the black sheen of the crow mid-day when he shoots across the sky to examine the latest addition to our compost pile. Life just wants to live, so the old saying goes, and this desire makes for tremendous innovation.

There is little script in this culture for such innovation when it comes to women's breasts. There is only the narrative everywhere I look of women made of curves and sleekness, women in clothing cut to highlight the roundness of breasts. Meanwhile, I feel like a 12-year-old with my bare chest cut so close to the bone. Meanwhile, the rest of my body blossoms so much older than the child I was. Meanwhile, the breasts in between past and present sleep on an invisible shelf.

I step outside again in the morning, the overgrown grass of early spring pouring over itself around the tilted cottonwood tree. The hills and wind around this home carry their own losses and scars, and yet are lit with a green both pale and fierce, quiet and shining, fully here at this moment and on the verge of changing completely. I return to earth and sky, continually coming home.

Chapter One: Getting Lost

We were completely lost in the Flint Hills of Kansas, and I didn't care. All we could see were the wide expanses of hills, sky, cows, and the occasional rock, skeleton of a windmill, or fragmented stones from pioneer homes. I stared out the front passenger side window, marveling at the lush green rising and falling in all directions, hardly any power lines because there was so little for the lines to power. The land looked surely as it had appeared for hundreds, thousands of years. Tall grass sloped all over itself on what felt like the top of the world, and everywhere the wind conspired with the sun to make the grasses gleam. It felt like being at very high altitude, only instead of mountains, windmills.

Expansive as galaxies, the Flint Hills lay down all directions like long, lanky bodies rolling away from or toward each other. "The sky begins at your feet," writes essayist Anne Herbert, and there's nothing like wandering around the center of Kansas to prove this, and also to find out how easy it is to get lost in the sky.

Early this March morning, the sun illuminated the curves of the land and long shadows of trees and rocks in such a way that we let ourselves get lost without a second thought. My friends and my nine-year-old daughter and I were driving all over Chase County, looking for the ranch of a woman we were to visit. We planned this trip the day before on a whim to make local contacts for the Continental Bioregional Congress we were helping to organize at a nearby camp the following fall. Now we were driving eight miles in the vibrant hills down the wrong road.

None of us spoke when we reached the dead-end. Instead, Joy just u-turned the car around, skimming some of the grass, and we headed back in the direction from which we came. We were all too taken with the sensation that this land went on forever, which conflicts with what I know of the prairie bioregion, a span of grasslands that stretches from western Missouri into eastern Colorado, north into Canada well past Winnipeg, and south into Mexico. Out of all the types of habitat on this continent, none is threatened with extinction as much as the prairie. Only 1% remains, the other 99% lost to development, farming, or erosion. The prairie left may be only a fragment of the original but it billows wide, framing a huge sky. Imagining the prairie when it was 100% intact is akin to imagining infinity, or at least, infinity divided into parcels of land.

I didn't know that once we righted ourselves, found the woman we were to meet, delighted in driving all over the county for a few more hours, and eventually made our way home, I would begin another kind of trip. I didn't know that while I was merrily lost, a technician from our local hospital's mammography department was leaving a message on my answering machine that I needed to come back for further x-rays. That further x-rays would lead to a biopsy with an old doctor, white-tufted and shaking his head, who would say, once he saw the mistletoe-shaped lump in my breast, "Yes, this looks very worrisome indeed."

I just knew how alive I felt, and how the world seemed, at that moment of being lost, to be forming anew, which, it turned out, was also true.

When I returned home, I casually tossed my bag on the chair, picked up the jacket one of my sons left on the floor, and glanced outside at the fields surrounding us and the woods in the distance. We—my husband, Ken, and our three kids—lived in a passive solar house we designed ourselves. The house, shaped like an angular crescent with eight more feet on the south side than the north, stood against the woods, which tilted upward to the east, toward a county park with an overlook named for Ken's grandfather. To the west of our home, the land sloped down to a tall grass prairie we'd been gradually restoring, mostly by burning it off each year. Although we only owned five acres outright, we dwelt on an island in family land: 130 or so acres of hackberry and cedar-filled woods, brome fields, and rectangles or squares of native prairie on land Ken used to farm. We were in the country, yet we were just three miles south of the city of Lawrence, and close enough to Highway 59 to hear the cicada-like drone of traffic, especially in winter when the trees were bare.

I drank a glass of water as I hit the play button on the answering machine. The dog, a laid-back black lab with Dalmatian patches, walked by sheepishly, trying not to show me she was carrying in her mouth one of my daughter's red-sparkle dress shoes, another treasure to bury in the couch. Outside the light was retreating, the western sky burning pink with fractured clouds filling the windows; inside, on the machine, a voice reminded me of a dental appointment, a friend explained why she wouldn't be able to make lunch on Thursday, and the radiologist, trying to sound professional and kind simultaneously, was saying there was a problem with my mammogram.

I played all the messages again, trying to understand what "new set of x-rays" meant although something in me already knew, and that voice was yelling, "Ken, Ken, come here quick!" I glanced around for the kids, and saw Natalie swinging outside, Daniel on the couch, reading a computer magazine wedged inside his algebra book, and Forest reading alongside Daniel.

They looked up briefly, and Forest smiled. "Mom, you're home!" he called out, but went back to an article on new video games. Ken came up slowly from the basement, a tall man who always moved thoughtfully.

"Hey, you're back," he said, kissing me and then opening the refrigerator to root around for a carrot.

"No, you have to come in the bedroom with me. Right now." He got his carrot and followed me to our bedroom, where we headed whenever the news or our tempers were bad. I curled up in the worn easy chair we had found months earlier on a street curb. He sat on the edge of our bed, leaning forward, asking with his hands what this was about. Although it was warm outside, I shivered.

"Something is wrong with my mammogram," I said, immediately crying.

"It's probably nothing," he tried to reassure me, looking over the top of his glasses. "It's probably just a lump. You said you had lumpy breasts." He sat opposite me as he spoke, looking both fully present and completely logical. It didn't work for me. I looked at him, his face always amazingly years younger than his age, his blue eyes unwavering in their devotion.

But it wasn't enough to keep me from tumbling toward a darkness that didn't seem to bottom out. Breast cancer ran in my family, but at 42, I didn't think it was on my menu for another decade or two.

I was also at the busiest point in my life between teaching, parenting, agitating, organizing, and writing. Just conveying to anyone what I "did" was itself a part-time job, but mostly, I could say I was an expert packer. I could pack up the back of our van for a camping trip, squeezing odd-shaped bags or angular coolers together without an inch of space wasted. I did the same with my time.

I taught in Goddard College's low-residency program, which meant I flew to Vermont twice a year and worked with students intensively via the mail. This work, the main way I made a living, also included ample work designing and co-creating the curriculum for a new academic field, Transformative Language Arts, which is all about using the written, spoken, and sung word for social and personal transformation. So I spent a lot of time emailing colleagues, working with students to each develop a community practicum, and revising handbooks and website material.

I served as the main coordinator for the Continental Bioregional Congress, the ecological event responsible for bringing the group of us to the Flint Hills the day before, and the first such congress to be organized in the last six years. The congress promised to gather activists, artists, farmers, builders, community leaders, educators, gardeners, and basically anyone from back-to-landers still planting the good garden to city administrators, puzzled over how to zone strawbale houses.

Ken and I co-led an eclectic group of farmers and activists who were fighting the state highway department over whether the nearby Highway 59, a dangerous county highway, should be widened slightly (our stance) or moved half a mile east and turned into a large freeway (their stance). In addition, I facilitated writing workshops for low-income women at the local housing authority. I also packed my life tightly enough to make time between work and three kids to huddle alone in coffee shops over my laptop, working on my own poetry and fiction, the kind of writing that I couldn't survive without doing.

Then there were the kids: Daniel, 12 at the time, was called "intense" by almost every teacher he ever had. Diagnosed with Asperger's Syndrome, a confusing made-up term that basically meant he meandered to the beat of his own inner pianist, Daniel was immersed in seventh grade and sat on the couch most of each weekend, reading *Far Side* cartoons and old *Mad* magazines. Lately, though, I'd told Ken I thought he was evolving out of this stage into the Monty Python developmental stage. Natalie, nine, busied herself with a constant parade of boyfriends and a sudden refusal to wear dresses after wearing nothing but dresses (the frillier the better) since she was two. Left to her own devices, she raised frogs in her room, drew Japanese animé, and sang.

Forest, just six years old, liked wrapping himself with fleece blankets and joining Daniel on the couch to pour over those old *Mads*, which is actually how he taught himself to read a year ago. The only laid-back child of our family, he tended to compensate for the rest of us by laughing out loud at the comics in the paper and wandering over to his grandparents' house on the other side of the hill, where he made them watch so many *Sponge Bob Squarepants* episodes that I'm sure they lost several years of good brain cells. All three kids took piano, went to Hebrew school, needed new shoes or special index cards for school, and had to be picked up or dropped off at a patchwork quilt of odd times. Because I mainly worked in front of my laptop and maintained flexible hours, I was the designated driver.

Added together, the life I led left no room whatsoever for even a mild cold, let alone a mild case of cancer.

"Let me research this. It'll make you feel better," Ken said, tapping my knee as he got up. Research might make him feel better, but I needed to talk. I called my mother in New Jersey, my old homeland after spending the earlier part of my life in Brooklyn. She had had breast cancer three or four years ago, a small lump that resulted in a small surgery and six weeks of radiation. Then it was all over.

She answered right away, and instinctively asked, "What's going on?" first.

"I flunked my mammogram."

"You what?"

"I got a mammogram, and I didn't pass it or something. I have to go back and do more x-rays."

She went silent.

"But you got your breast cancer after menopause, right? And most women my age don't get breast cancer."

She was still quiet.

"Besides, I have lumpy breasts, so it's probably nothing," I said, trying to convince myself.

She asked when I went in for the x-rays, told me to call her right away, and sighed but didn't say much more.

Later that evening, Ken reported that only 20% of biopsies (and we weren't even at the biopsy stage yet) were problems. At work—he was an occupational therapist at a state facility for the developmentally disabled—he had met some women who had breast cancer, and lots of others who had bad mammograms that proved to be harmless. So what was the chance of me having a problem?

The chance got larger after we sat in the hospital waiting room a few days later, me snapping at him for telling me I had bad breath when I was so stressed out, and him trying to reason, unreasonably, with me. After I was called back to the mammography machines, big animals that metallically lunged at my breasts, twisting them upward and pulling in as much of my chest wall as possible, I met another technician who said there was a pattern, a line of calcium deposits, that could be "of concern," and I would need to see a surgeon for a biopsy. I stared at the x-ray with him, both of us pointing to the curved line of white specks. A classic pattern of breast cancer, I would learn later, but for now, it looked like a photograph of a constellation. I thought of how much Ken loved astronomy.

A few days later, the surgeon had me lie down on the table, and with his large hands put the cold mouth of what looked like a microphone on the side of my left breast. The heat in my face and the ache in my stomach made me think I already knew. So I wasn't surprised when he showed me something on the screen that looked like a flame, asymmetrical, white against the black background, while the nurse held my hand and nodded. Then he placed a kind of medical gun against the outside of my left breast, and shot it into me, extracting first one, then another sample of the tumor.

"It's cancer probably, isn't it?" I asked the nurse. She tried to not answer and still be sympathetic, but she knew, too.

Waiting for the doctor's call the next morning, I was ready to leave my body and reside elsewhere. The kids were home for spring break, crowded around the miniature television set (just five inches across) on the kitchen table, watching *Arthur's* antics on PBS. I tried to wash the counter, but felt too scared to stay in the same space with them. The best I could do was to go to the basement, boot up my computer, and start answering emails. Every phone call made me jump hysterically. Ken was at work in Topeka, 40 minutes away, but he would meet me at the doctor's if we needed to go there. We would only need to be there to get the news in person if it was bad news. Otherwise a nurse could just say, "Oh, it's no problem."

The phone call finally came. It was the nurse, "The doctor would like to see you. Can you come in at 11?" It was still spring break, all three of my all-too-lively and too-young-to-be-left-alone kids home from school.

"Of course," I answered. "It's bad then?"

"Yes, it's cancer, but you already knew that." She had a reassuring voice, practiced at being loving in moments like this.

I tried to call my in-laws to have them watch the kids, but they were gone. I called a bunch of friends, one after the other, and no one was home. I called Judy, my closest friend, on her cell phone, but she was out of town and could only say that she loved me as she raced down I-70. I ended up leaving a message on the machine of someone I didn't know well, asking her to come out and watch the kids.

I ran upstairs and looked at my kids. They were finishing off a box of frozen waffles, getting syrup all over the table, and still watching *Arthur* and his annoying sister. They hardly looked up when I quietly explained, trying to keep the earthquake inside me hidden, that they would be staying by themselves for the first time because I had a doctor's appointment, nothing to worry about. Besides, Grandma and Grandpa would be home soon. They may have vaguely nodded at me, but I was already out the door, racing down the drive, crying on and off, feeling like an enormous force just drop-kicked me in the stomach.

I arrived before Ken and was quickly escorted into the doctor's office without even 10 minutes to read through the newest news magazines neatly piled on the small table in the waiting room. Dr. Lewis sat opposite me behind the large, worn wooden desk that took up most of the room, and spoke while I scribbled notes in my journal. I had remembered once reading something about the importance of taking notes at moments like this. The room seemed dark to me although it was probably a light color.

He began. It was two things: invasive ductal carcinoma, the most common kind of breast cancer, and DCIS, which I found out later was cancerous cells having a cocktail party in the duct system, not officially on a rampage yet. "Most of the time, the cancer gets into the blood very early," he explained to me. I didn't quite understand yet that this would translate into a word I had vowed never to get cozy with chemotherapy. Having watched my mother and aunt each have a lumpectomy and radiation, I thought I would simply give six weeks to this expedition, as they had done.

Ken came and sat next to me as I obediently wrote down everything the doctor said, afraid to look at Ken for fear I would lose my business-like demeanor that kept everything suspended above reality just enough. He was afraid to look at me, too. The doctor thought the tumor was only about 6 millimeters large, and they would need to remove a lump the size of a golf ball from my left breast. I thought of magicians pulling ping pong balls from people's ears to the crowd's astonishment.

The doctor went on to speak about how aggressive breast cancer was in pre-menopausal women like myself. A new procedure, the sentinel lymph node biopsy, would inject dye and radioactive fluid into my lymph nodes to see if any lit up like they were part of a cancer pinball machine. Or I could choose to do the ancillary lymph node dissection, where my lymph nodes would simply be cut out, just to be sure; whatever I wanted for the side dish, as long as a lumpectomy was the main course.

"A lot of people will tell you all kinds of things about cancer, but if you have questions, you come back to me," the doctor said gently. "I study this all the time so I really have answers for you." I nodded, numb and efficient, and answered the questions he asked about my work, my kids; questions to show he could see me as a person, not just a six-millimeter morsel of invasive ductal carcinoma.

Afterwards, Ken and I stood up and shook his soft hand, stepped out of the room and immediately saw the nurse who hugged me and filled my arms with handouts about support groups and mastectomy supplies. We walked closely, holding hands but not saying much until we got to our cars, both of us shuddering without knowing it yet. Surgery was set for Tuesday, three days later. The doctor, who was left-handed, and his associate, who was right-handed, would do the surgery together, a double-animal with lots of experience. We both were reassured by how fast this would be resolved.

The parking lot seemed larger, and the sky, darkening to the west, seemed more overcast. Amazingly, I walked right to where I parked the car, drawn to it like magnet to magnet.

Ken leaned down to kiss me as I put my key in the lock. "See you at home," he said, and then I got in. I watched him crossing to his car, his hands deep in his pockets, his head down.

I sat in the van, picked up the cell phone, and called my mother.

"Shit," she said.

I phoned Judy, a fellow New York Jew in Kansas, or "yid in the mid" as we liked to joke. A Buddhist who meditated early each morning, she listened carefully.

"Oh, baby," she said.

I called Victoria, another best friend, a Kansas native who, back when we were in our twenties, would join me in over-analyzing every aspect of our emotional lives while complaining that people found us too intense. We'd given up our intensity, me for kids, and her for the Greek Orthodox Church.

"I'll pray for you," she said.

I drove home, and found out that the friend I had called did indeed show up to watch the kids. Ken and I took the children over to my in-laws' house for a few hours, went home and lay down beside each other in the bedroom, holding on tight. It was mid-day, a time we were usually separated by work. The air outside was deliciously spring-like. But we were entering a different sort of season, and we had no idea what the weather was like or how long we'd live there.

Chapter Two:
Falling into a
Big Vat of Butter

Peggy, an old friend who grew up in Texas, once said to me, "Coming to Lawrence, Kansas, is like falling in a big vat of butter." Peggy herself would eventually be diagnosed with breast cancer that metastasized and ended her life too early, but at the time she said this to me—sometime in the late 1980s—I knew exactly what she meant.

In 1982, a friend and I were traveling from Kansas City to the first bioregional gathering of the Kansas Area Watershed Council, at a camp 50 miles away. We were talking so much that we kept missing the I-70 exit west from Kansas City. When we finally found our way, we were tired so we decided to stop in Lawrence. Soon, we found ourselves dancing at a small concert of a local band named Tofu Teddy, going out for Mexican food afterwards, and then staying overnight at a friend of a friend's house in East Lawrence.

Walking up the steps of this old bungalow, I had a sensation unlike anything before or since: I felt the presence of someone saying, from just over my right shoulder, "This is your home for the rest of your life." It was my first visit to Lawrence, and the next day I met Ken and many people who were to become my closest friends. Within a year, I moved to Lawrence and just kept falling deeper into the buttery ease of the community.

This is all by way of saying that, when I was diagnosed with cancer, I had a lot of people to call. But all the phone calls didn't make the cancer any more real for me.

At first, it felt as if I was taking notes and making contacts for a good friend whom I loved dearly, and who faced a life-threatening illness and would now have to decide the best form of treatment. My denial was so deep that when I spoke to close friends, I could feel acutely their point of view rather than my own.

Ken and I told the kids one night after dinner, which as usual consisted of a hodge-podge of multiple choices. (We consistently failed at the kind of parenting that resulted in obedient children and single-meal dinners.) After clearing the salad, ramen noodles, left-over pasta with pesto, and a half-eaten hamburger, we called them back to the table and said we needed to talk to them. They came reluctantly, returning to their seats and looking puzzled.

"What we have to tell you," Ken said, looking mostly at Natalie, who seemed on the verge of tears simply because of him talking like this, "is that your mom has breast cancer, but it's caught early, and she's going to be okay."

Daniel tried to stand up but made himself sit down again. Forest just listened and nodded.

"She's going to need surgery to take the cancer out, and then she'll probably need some medicine." I winced at this. "Or some other kind of treatment, but it'll probably just take a few months, and then she'll be okay."

"Oh, no! What if the cancer spreads through her body? What if it's spread already and starting to attack her organs? It could be metastasizing right now," Daniel said. I was sorry we had kept so many science magazines around the house all these years.

Natalie's small face turned red, and she stared at the spilled ketchup on the table. I reached out and hugged her sideways toward me, but she was rigid and far away.

"Sorry about the cancer, Mom," said Forest, his dark blue eyes shining, "and, um, could I have an ice cream bar?" I nodded, gestured for him to bring me one too.

"Why do bad things keep happening to our family?" Natalie asked. Just twelve months before, a car accident had injured Forest, and the memory of that event was still fresh in everyone's mind.

I didn't know, so I lied. "It's not so bad. I mean, we got through the accident without anyone being hurt too badly, and now we'll get through this okay too."

She stared at me, her large brown eyes burning right through whatever I said. Ken pulled her onto his lap, put his long arm around her, and she huddled into him.

The whole time we talked to them I was convinced this wasn't happening to my kids' mother, but rather to someone sort of like her who dressed a little nicer and did a better job of cleaning the kitchen, a close friend who didn't deserve this.

Within a few days, I also emailed the news to several groups Ken and I were involved with. The Continental Bioregional Congress group was composed mainly of my oldest friends from Lawrence. The Highway 59 group was a coalition Ken and I had brought together with another couple, Retta and Ozzie. I also emailed fellow faculty members, my students, my women's writing group, and other friends near and far.

"I have cancer," I typed onto the screen or said into the phone receiver dozens of times. "Cancer, yeah, it's breast cancer." I felt like a character on a mediocre television sit-com.

I called Courtney and Denise, a lesbian couple in their twenties who were more like family to us since I officiated at their wedding a few years earlier. Denise had been through her own bout with thyroid cancer. She answered the phone, listened, and burst into loud wails. Courtney got on the line, and I tried to explain again, but I could hear her crying too. I was once again so removed from my own reality that their reactions seemed amazing to me.

It seemed like all I did for the first few days was sleep, stare at food like it was a strange substance sent down from Martians, and tell people on the phone, in the street, over email that I had cancer. Meanwhile, I was trying all the time to make it real, to make it count, to see what it meant for when I finally showed up for my own life.

All the time, I was floating above my own reactions, watching them unfold like a panorama. Fear burrowed underground. Courage slept in the corner next to the cat. Anxiety sat at a computer typing like a maniac. Hope looked out the window. Confusion tried to reprogram its VCR. Depression was leaning back on the couch, reading old *People* magazines. And there was me all the over the place.

In the haze of phone calls, one of the first numbers I dialed was Ursula's, a friend who made her living as an energy healer. No matter that she was in Germany at the time visiting her mother, I wanted my voice to be on her machine for her to hear as soon as she returned, and no wonder, considering what she had done for our family after the car accident a year earlier. I had hit a patch of black ice on the way to deposit all three kids at school during the single year that they were all in the same elementary school. Although I was surrounded by wide flat fields, the car threw itself off the road in the only place there was a ditch, flipping over.

Forest was life-flighted to the Kansas City children's hospital with his brain bleeding in three places, his lower face broken in five. I took the cell phone a passer-by handed me and called Ursula from the ambulance where the other kids were ready to be transported, each strapped to a board and terrified.

"Please, there's been a terrible accident," I told her, and within minutes, she was at the local hospital with us. Within hours, she was driving us to Kansas City to be with Forest. During the three days he spent in a drug-induced coma to prevent any further brain injuries, she was constantly by his side, holding him and doing the impossible-to-explain energy healing that saved his life.

At the end of the three days, the doctor carried in the latest x-rays, and told us, "I don't know what happened. My whole office is baffled. It's like he's another kid." The bleeding in his brain had stopped and all the breaks in his face, except for a minor hairline fracture, had disappeared. "We can't explain it," the doctor told us.

But knowing Ursula, who had been a healer for 40 years, and knowing how many friends and families had prayed, in every religion and in spiritual yearnings of their own invention, it was clear to me what was behind this miracle.

Now, two days after the official diagnosis, on a cold and gray Sunday morning, Ursula called me back, having returned from Germany. She sounded worried and said we needed to talk immediately. Twenty minutes later, she walked through our front door. Since the kids were making copious amounts of noise, I put my coat on, and Ursula and I walked into the big silver-gray field, the cold searing my cheeks. I looked for deer in the distance, along the hedge rows, but all I saw were a few errant vultures.

In the middle of the field, I turned to Ursula. She was wearing a thick green coat, her white hair huddled around her face for warmth. Older than me by a generation, and far shyer than I had ever been, she hung back at parties, sitting quietly against a wall and sipping hot water with lemon. It took me several years to get to know her. I would go over, sit beside her quietly, and ask her how she was. It was clear to me that she was the real deal, a true healer, and someone so sensitive to all sensations that I could tell she could barely stand groups, crowds, or parties.

"I don't even feel like I have cancer," I said, matter-of-factly.

Her blue eyes flared. "You have cancer," she said with great intensity.

The grass shone gray cold. Then Ursula informed me that a psychic entity she had consulted told her I should wait a few weeks to have the surgery, and that I should find another surgeon to do it. "The cancer is like a bee hive in you now," she said. "If they cut into it right away, it will explode into the body. You need to do some treatment first, get yourself ready, and then have the surgery."

The color flew out of me. "But we're supposed to do the surgery right away," I said, although I could feel in some pit deep inside myself that she was right.

I ran back to the house, and told Ken to get his coat so Ursula could tell him too. He looked as stunned as I felt. "But we have to do surgery now," he said. Yet Ursula had reinforced what already I knew: that the medical treadmill, the one that you stepped onto without knowing how fast it moved, was moving too quickly even for me, a person who tended to do all things fast.

Ken looked at me as if I were crazy, but as he put on his coat, his expression changed to a mixture of pain and fatigue. I took his hand, and we headed across the field to Ursula, who explained it all as he nodded, far too quiet. He stared at the old growth grass from last spring, bleached of its color.

"Okay," he said.

After she left, Ken and I closed our door and collapsed onto our bed. We were exhausted and confused about how to tell people that we were delaying the surgery because a group of channeled entities had told us, via Ursula, to do so. It was hard enough to explain Ursula.

But telling people was easier than I imagined. I simply said that I didn't feel that I had enough time to absorb any of this, and I wanted a few weeks to get myself ready and find someone who specialized in breast surgery. Even my mother immediately applauded this decision, thinking it was particularly astute to get an expert.

I sat up and did what I had avoided until now: I called my father, who was distant from me, both emotionally and geographically. He answered the phone with his usual, "What's up?" We had talked somewhat regularly for five or ten minutes at a time, over the years. But we had hardly shared more than the headlines of our lives since I had moved out at 19, often slip-sliding into fights that ended with one of us vowing never to speak to the other again.

"I had a mammogram, and...."

"A what? I can't hear you," he said in his strong Brooklyn accent.

"A mammogram. The test when they see if you have breast cancer. And I do. But it's found early, it should be okay, and I'm going to have surgery soon...I think."

"You have cancer?" Having grown up in a house where female body parts were never mentioned, it was awkward for me to even say the word "breast" to him.

"Yeah, I have cancer. But they found it early."

"Well, that's good. When's the surgery?"

"I don't know, but I'll call you as soon as I do. We're shopping around for a good doctor, a real expert," I added, knowing that he would approve.

"Don't let just anyone operate on you. Make sure you get the best," he answered, complying immediately.

"Yeah, that's what we're doing."

He paused, not knowing what to say. No one in his family had had cancer except his brother, Howard, who had died five years earlier from pancreatic cancer. I waited for him to say, "What you gonna do?" his trademark statement for life's mystery. But he didn't say anything else but goodbye.

That afternoon, we hosted a bioregional congress meeting in our living room, sitting with our friends, more solemn than usual, while the cold pressed up against the windows. Someone put up the easel and a giant pad so that everyone could go over the agenda. Written in red, toward the middle of the paper, was "Caryn's cancer," something we would have to deal with as a group. It fell squarely in the middle of the 18-month-time-span when we were meeting monthly and I was working daily to bring together hundreds of people concerned with ecology and culture for a week-long gathering.

Our planning group met once a month for three-hour sessions, so well-organized from all the facilitation training we had been through that the time went quickly and tended to make us more awake and also more hungry. We usually ended with a long, lingering potluck, visiting around the table or in the living room, or, when it was warm, outside around the table on the deck.

"Okay," said Ken. "We thought we could start with fund raising and then...."

"Wait," said Rita. "I don't feel like we can just go on like everything's normal." Rita was so committed to this event that she actually flew in to attend the monthly planning meetings from California where she lived on a limited budget with her life partner, Rachel, and two very energetic dogs. A fifty-ish woman with short hair, large breasts, and a helluva singing voice, Rita found us a few years ago through an email and had quickly turned into someone who seemed to have been a friend for decades. "I mean, Caryn has cancer, and I just can't stand this. It's so unfair. All these friends of mine are getting cancer, and it's...."

I sat in the wooden rocking chair, steeling myself, frozen from the inside out as I listened. Rita was crying so hard that she couldn't talk. As I circled the room with my eyes, I saw everyone else was crying too. Jerry, one of my closest and absolutely my quietest friend, was holding our new kitten, his eyes red and watching me. Joy too had tears running down her cheeks. I had first met her two decades ago while we were learning energy conservation techniques in a local junkyard, when she was a skinny girl with long braids and I was more New Yorker than Midwesterner. I heard Ken crying, but I knew I couldn't make eye contact with him without slamming into a wall of pain.

"It's like the earth," Rita managed to say.

I nodded. It was exactly like the earth, which, as Stephanie Mills writes, "perfectly bespeaks us." Ken and I had already talked, late at night when I couldn't sleep, which was often these days, about how the environmental poisons couldn't help but affect our health. Research was now starting to reflect these deeper and more pervasive causes of cancer. Just last night, as I pulled on my nightgown, Ken told me, "It's like uncontrolled growth."

"Cancer, you mean?"

"Yeah. It's exactly like the Highway 59 fight. We're trying to stave off the kind of uncontrolled growth that destroys an ecosystem."

I thought of my body now as its own ecosystem. The land we were trying to protect in the highway fight was laden with historic markers, such as the wagon train ruts from the Santa Fe Trail, and very probably a Native American burial site. There were virgin woods and native prairie. The land was like me, I thought, like my body bearing the marks of loss as well as places still young and healthy, and places threatened with development. My breasts harbored the agents of suburban sprawl.

The back door opened, and Curtis and a friend entered, having just driven here from Oklahoma, and as usual, arriving late. Curtis half-smiled, flipped his curly hair out of his face, and said, with his strong Oklahoma accent and in a tone that implied that whatever looked bad couldn't possibly be, "This looks kinda heavy."

"It is," someone replied. When Rita told him that I had cancer, he deflated and sank into the couch. His friend, a young woman named Sara, happened to be wearing a button with a photo of woman's chest, after a mastectomy. I glanced over at her button every so often during the meeting, feeling reassured by the strength of the image and also downright scared of the strength I would need to grow in myself.

Eventually, the meeting got underway, and I agreed to take a few months off while others picked up some of my tasks. We went over fundraising efforts, and whether we could ask local organizations to donate $100 each to become cosponsors. We talked about who would track down mailing lists we could use, and if it were possible to prepare a website soon.

As usual, we finished with a large potluck, sitting together at a table laden with Russian peasant soup, brownies, home made bread, coleslaw, and chips. But nothing broke through to me until everyone was leaving and Jerry hugged me. He was the same height as me, his heart beating right into mine. We stood there for a long time, holding each other, each breath we took together telling me I had cancer, but I had friends, too. I let myself fall into it.

Chapter Three:
Divining for Doctors
and Dharma

Archie Bunker and Dr. Doolittle

When I called a Kansas City hospital that sported a breast cancer clinic, I was told that I couldn't see the nationally-renowned oncologist some friends recommended—she wasn't taking on any new patients—but I could consult with a Dr. Doolittle and an Archibald Bunker.

"So you've got Dr. Doolittle and Archie Bunker?" Judy asked me on the phone. I was washing the kitchen counter, trying to get dried mustard off the stainless steel that wasn't so stainless. Judy was driving west to meet Zen Buddhist students in another town.

"Yeah, but I'm not so sure about Doolittle," I answered, puttering toward my home's greenhouse where I was suddenly planting everything I could get my hands on that involved blossoms. "I mean, he talks to the animals."

"And I would think seriously about Archie Bunker also," she replied. "You know what a bigot he is."

I visited Dr. Bunker anyway, and did it alone since Ken couldn't get off work, confident that I could get all my questions answered and determine if he was indeed the surgeon of my dreams. But when I got there, after waiting for the doctor for over an hour, I instead met a beautiful African-American resident with an explosion of braids and a great smile. She went over all the usual questions of family history, health history, and when I was diagnosed, and she had me lie down on the table, my arm over my head, while she pressed down with two fingers on my breast, out from the center, over and over until the whole breast was covered. She would be one of what seemed like dozens of doctors and residents doing breast exams on me for months to come.

Dr. Bunker was small, dark-haired and light-eyed, which gave him the appearance of a short Robert DeNiro. I had a flood of questions, but first he told me we would probably do a special procedure, performed only here and two other places in the country, where a catheter was put into my breast after the surgery, and then radiation was injected right into the breast, eliminating some of the radiation time needed later on. He assured me it was a great way to wipe out any cancer cells locally with minimal side effects. Then he said something about my needing to be quarantined for three days for this procedure.

Dr. Bunker said he had lots of experience with the new sentinel lymph node procedure, and assured me that it would be enough. But he didn't have more than a few minutes, despite me being there for over two hours already. Before I got even a few of my questions out, he was gone, and I was back with the resident. My mind was spinning at the idea of having some contraption put into my breast, something that I immediately envisioned as miniature aliens, the kind spied in the *Men in Black* movies.

"Oh, I forgot to examine your breasts," he said, rushing back.

He did so quickly as I lay there staring at the ceiling, feeling his smaller, cool fingers search for something more than the breast's normal inhabitants. Then he was gone again. But he seemed so clear and efficient, like someone who could probably pluck tumors from breasts in his sleep. Choosing him meant my search would be over soon after it began, which felt happily reassuring. I smiled, relaxed a little.

Pulling out of the parking lot, I handed the attendant, an older woman with a gray cloud of hair around her black face, my card, certified by the cancer clinic.

"Oh, baby," she said. "You're too young for this."

Chemo, the Barbarian

"You've got to see Matt Stein," said Martha, a woman a few decades older than me who had a determined voice that conveyed that she had seen it all. We were standing in the social hall of the Jewish Community Center, where she had just finished describing her mastectomy a decade earlier. The center, housed in a building that could be the poster child for the ugly and poor-quality construction of the seventies, was something we inexplicably clung to, stubbornly refusing to even consider rebuilding it.

"Matt Stein is the best," said Ron, an attorney from Iowa who looked like his ancestors swam in the same gene pool as mine. "Oh, he's a doll. I'm enthralled with him," added Jeannette, a Mexican-American convert who made the best cakes on the planet and who had just tunneled through her own breast cancer. "He's a god among men," piped Janice, who had recently finished chemo for colon cancer and was sporting tight new curls—"the chemo perm," she called it.

Our kids had joined a large bunch of others kids, and the multiplication of children made for loud shrieks and grapes smashed into the floor around us. Occasionally, one of us—parent or not—would tell the kids to settle down, keep the food out of the sanctuary, and ask for help pouring juice, but mostly the kids had free rein, and they knew it.

We had just sung our way together through Friday night services, and when the rabbi asked for names for the Misheberech, a prayer for healing of the ailing, my name was spoken. It would be like this for many months to come, every Friday night a prayer sung for me and others, sometimes with someone's hand on my shoulder. This was my religious community, a place I felt at home, and sometimes, as a New York Jew living in the wilds of Kansas, the only place. When my people spoke, they said "Matt Stein" to me enough that I knew he would be my oncologist even before I met him.

Dr. Stein was tall and urgent about all things relating to cancer. He could also talk fast. Sitting at a round table in a small conference room with Ken, a pile of cancer.gov documents that Ken had generated in front of us, Dr. Stein spun off a pile of information about protocols, explained my lab report to me, handed me copies of everything he could get his hands on from other doctors about me, and gave a detailed description of various treatments. There was something about his voice that immediately felt familiar.

We continued plowing through all the potential details while he had me put on a hospital gown and lie down. Then he examined my breasts, unable to feel any lump. I tried to pretend this was normal, one doctor after another looking at and pressing his fingers along my previously private body parts. Looking at the ceiling and talking about medical studies helped.

But the only thing I heard from my first conversation with him was that even if I didn't have any lymph node involvement, I would need chemo, four rounds, 12 weeks. I couldn't help thinking of Genghis Khan, whom I had written about years before—my first book contract (although a fight between two of my editors resulted in my contract being canceled and the book unpublished). Still, what I'd learned of Khan and his men who killed an average of 500 people a year over decades—all of the deaths brutal, most unwarranted—made me wonder if the chemo would operate like this, beating, burning, beheading every errant cell it met.

I tried to keep nodding, trying to appear as if I was listening despite the flashes of wild terror that echoed through my body. I mean, I was a person who couldn't handle anything stronger than aspirin. I couldn't even drink a beer without getting a migraine. I couldn't handle cold medicine, for goodness sake. How could I survive the terminator-strength potency of chemotherapy?

"Chemotherapy is a form of brutality," Dr. Stein said as he squeezed my hand. "I won't lie to you about that, but for now, it's the best we have."

I pretended to take notes while Ken asked question after question he had devised after reading who-knows-how-many pages from the cancer.gov website. "How would we know the chemo works?"

"Only in retrospect," said Dr. Stein.

Ken went on with his list of questions: What is the usual protocol, and why might we try another one? What about the new hormone-based therapies? Could I work? What would happen to my energy level? Would I be able to sleep at night? What are the statistics for effectiveness of radiation plus chemo versus just chemo? Did he recommend a port be installed in me as a way to lessen the chance of the chemo causing skin damage?

I felt like a space shuttle being readied for repairs, while in reality I was just a body with one overriding worry: nausea. Dr. Stein explained that nausea mostly could be controlled, but there would be other potential and common side effects, such as fatigue, hair loss, mouth sores, diarrhea, constipation, depression. Considering I got nauseous at the possibility of nausea, when he read off the list, I started to feel not only nauseous, but a little depressed and deeply tired.

There was also the question of whether I had something called BRCA 1 or 2, a breast cancer genetic defect that implied skyscraper-high risks of breast and ovarian cancers and if so, whether I wanted to have a double mastectomy and a word it took me six months to learn how to pronounce: an oophorectomy, which meant removal of the ovaries. Getting tested for BRCA would take weeks, so how long should I wait for surgery, or should I have surgery right away and then get tested?

The Mongolian army was strong, but I was stopped at a crossroads, not sure which way the enemy was or what beloved territory would be left after all this. I pondered whether to turn to macrobiotics, prayer on mountain tops, or mistletoe injections in Germany instead.

Finally, I leaned forward and looked into Dr. Stein's eyes. "What would you do if I was your wife?"

He leaned forward too, looked intently at me, and said, "If you were my wife, I'd say to get the surgery right now since I like to have all the information I can have before deciding what to do. After surgery, we'll know a lot more about your cancer."

After two hours with Dr. Stein, Ken and I took our spinning minds and hungry bodies to lunch at an upscale restaurant.

Chemo, chemo, chemo, was all I thought as Ken and I sat down in a dimly-lit booth with a small candle in the center. I ordered a fish stew, something with a French name full of things I loved: mussels, shrimp, scallops, and a lot of garlic. But even as I put a forkful of this delicious stuff into my mouth, and Ken and I joked about Dr. Doolittle treating two-headed giraffes, all I could hear in the back of my head was the chemo chant.

"Hey," Ken said, trying to distract me, "at least your oncologist will be a god among men."

Exotic Flowers

It was one of those delicious April nights, just a tinge cool and filled with the smell of spring almost here. I had stopped at Ursula's to say hi on my way home from picking up more vitamins. She opened the door radiating this one message: "I know exactly who you need to see! Amie Jew, she's a great surgeon." Dr. Jew was a breast surgeon at Menorah Medical Center in Kansas City, and she was also particularly open to other kinds of healing.

"Is her name really 'Jew'?" It was, which made telling people about her an act of delivering a punch line: "You know, her name is Amie Jew, so she has to be my surgeon." Everyone laughed that this was a match made in heaven. The fact that she was at a Jewish hospital made the deal even more entrancing. I was delighted and sure that the connection of her name and my religion was written in the stars.

Amie Jew's office was full of exotic flowers and some great magazines on simple but elegant ways to beautify your home. I read through them, feeling ashamed of how messy my own house was. Then I pulled out a packet from Elaine, a Goddard student who was designing a writing group for rural high school students that combined ecology and yoga. I marveled at Elaine's beautiful essay on taking a herd of 16-year-olds on a walk in the woods, pausing to do downward dog or mountain pose.

When they called my name, Ken and I leapt up and went to a back room where we waited. We had paper and pen in hand, and by then I was in the little half-hospital gown that opened in the back, waiting for yet another person to touch my breasts.

Dr. Jew, a small Chinese-American woman with her long hair pulled back and a string of elegant pearls, smiled and shook our hands. She was delighted that we knew Ursula, and she had a lot to say about every possible question we harbored. No, she told us, a sentinel node dissection is not enough. She herself had refused to be part of a national trial because while the people who pioneered it had a 95% effectiveness rate, she seriously doubted whether everyone using this relatively new technique was as effective. She drew pictures on her note pad, using curves and flat lines, showing us what all our options were: simple mastectomy, radical mastectomy, or lumpectomy. She talked at length about recovery time, and the need to move the arms afterwards to make sure that I didn't lose any range of motion, particularly since she would be cutting close to muscle.

As she talked, I realized I would have to give up attending a conference I was looking forward to as well as forgoing some other events, but to my surprise, I didn't care. In fact, I felt somewhat relieved to let another part of my life slough off and fall away.

After 90 minutes with her, Ken and I were completely convinced that she was our surgeon. Her office made us an appointment to meet Dr. Sanders, the radiologist with whom Dr. Jew insisted we consult before she set a surgery date. We left, marveling at the beautiful multi-layered inner garden the hospital was built around. We had a surgeon, an oncologist, and now we just had to go paint-by-number toward a surgery date.

Dr. Sanders could have been a fashion model, if he wasn't so busy shooting rays of nuclear power through people's bodies. He sat down with us in an examining room and did something that bowled us over with admiration: before he said a word, he asked me to describe all I knew about my situation. By gauging his comments to ours, he then launched into an explanation of the cancer without telling us what we already knew. He said that breast cancer tumors doubled in size every 210 days, on average. He explained that the constellation of calcium spots were waste products of a tumor. We went over the tumor measurement, and he said I had a slow-growing tumor, and that radiation should kill all cancer cells in the breast for up to five years. The radiation would lower my chance of recurrence by only an additional 1%, but that was still significant.

When he examined my breasts, pressing his fingers in the same way as the other doctors had, he looked at my face. "You know, my wife had breast cancer, stage three by the time we found it."

"Wow, that must have been terrifying," I said.

"It was, especially knowing what I know about cancer. It changes your whole life to go through something like this." He paused, then started pressing on my belly, probably making sure no tumors had headed south. "She's fine now, at least we think she is, but it made me understand what it's like to know you might lose someone, and there's nothing you can do to stop it."

I watched his face and felt such relief to meet a doctor who had been through this himself, who knew firsthand the uncertainty, the tidal waves of fear, the yearning to make it right. "So," he said, encouraging me to sit up, "how do you do with drugs usually?"

I bolted upright, told him how easily I threw up, and how bad an idea chemo was for me. After all, my whole childhood was spent traveling with bags in my lap for when I inevitably would vomit in the back seat of the station wagon while going over one of the bridges spanning the Hudson River or past a rest stop on the New Jersey turnpike.

Then he said something that gave me back my nerve: he told me details of a study in Vietnam about how removing the ovaries works just as well in preventing recurrence as undergoing chemotherapy. Months of poisons pumped through my body or a little laparoscopic surgery to suck out my ovaries? It wasn't much of a contest.

"But this is only possible if you're stage one," he added, meaning if the cancer hadn't traveled to my lymph nodes.

"I'm sure I am only stage one," I told him. So were all my friends, so it had to be true. He even agreed that it was likely, given how tiny this tumor was, that every bit was contained in one bad seed that would soon be lifted out of me and discarded.

The rest of the day I spent telephoning people with the great news: I could trade my ovaries for chemo. It would be over in a flash, and I would be back to my life pronto, a little altered, a little more sensitive perhaps to what cancer meant, but not really changed. The cancer would be like a display of deadly exotic flowers that flash their vibrancy for a while, and eventually end up in the compost heap.

Download and Dharma

Although Ken had been downloading piles of information from websites, I wasn't ready to read any of it until now. One evening after getting the kids to bed, I picked up the pile and started looking at statistics, charts, new drug trial information, chemo regimens.

Mostly, I read the descriptions of chemo side effects. I had kept my unruly hair short for years, and now it would be gone. I wondered, sitting on my bed one night to go through the material, if I would turn out to have a lopsided head. The idea of a wig sounded claustrophobic, not to mention hot during the sauna-like Kansas summer.

One study I looked at detailed the rise of breast cancer over the last 40 years, how it used to be one in 12 women, then one in 10, and now it was one in eight. Would it be one in two by the end of my life? Then, even thinking of the word, "end," made me shiver and put down the papers. I knew Ken had been looking at environmental studies on breast cancer.

Lumpectomy surgery was two weeks away, set for April 19th. I had been busy taking vitamins and herbs to strengthen myself; turning the greenhouse in our house into a miniature healing temple of sorts, complete with all the cards people sent posted on the walls. I had made detailed arrangements about where the kids would be and who would pick them up from school and deposit them at various activities, happy with my illusion of order in the world.

Ken came into our bedroom, sat on the floor leaning against our bed. "We're waiting too long to do the surgery," he said. "This is going to happen almost a month after you were diagnosed." He had his arms folded across his chest and was shaking his head. His mouth was a straight line.

The waiting didn't scare me.

"And you don't have any life insurance," he reminded me. Just three months before the cancer, we had agreed to get me some life insurance, and I had found a great plan on the internet—$25 a month for $400,000 in insurance—but being as busy as I was, I didn't take the time to return the email and fill out the forms. "No one is going to insure you now."

I looked at his face and knew he was imagining the worst: what it would be like to raise three kids without me, what it would mean to raise them on his salary, which, although it was more than mine, wasn't enough on its own. Mostly, he was imagining the wild and consuming grief that would come for him if I died, the look on his face traveling from anger into the pain beneath it and then back to anger.

Daniel burst into the room. "Forest is being a complete jerk, and you need to do something about it now!"

Natalie came in on his heels. "It's not Forest, it's Daniel. I saw it all, and Daniel is lying."

Forest, free of both of them, was back in the living room, reading the magazine he and Daniel had been fighting over.

"We're trying to talk here. Work it out yourselves," I said.

"Just take turns. Now go, and close the door."

For whatever reason, they did.

I turned back to Ken. "I guess," I said slowly, "this means I just can't die." We both would normally giggle as this kind of humor, but we weren't laughing now. He sighed and looked down.

Meanwhile, I was getting floods of emails from colleagues, friends, people I hardly knew. Leon called from San Francisco to tell me about Marge, who had breast cancer 20 years ago. "She died, you know," he added.

Linda, visiting from Tennessee, called to say, "Mammograms cause cancer, and that's why I'm not getting one, and why you probably got cancer in the first place." Carol wrote to me about blue-green algae. Theodore sent articles about macrobiotics. Someone sent me an article about having the fillings in my teeth removed.

While I knew all these people were well-intentioned, I found I needed to stop answering the phone and be very careful when I opened an email to hit the delete button quickly on occasion. Otherwise, I would feel overrun by intruders, distracting me from actually dealing with the cancer on my own level and in my own way. Yet it became remarkably obvious to me how much cancer was a trigger for the wounds of multitudes, and how few of them realized that what they were saying was for them, not me.

Most of all, I was downloading my own submerged fears into my walk-a-day existence. Why, I thought, as all cancer survivors must think at one time, did I have cancer? Why me and not the man who starved a batch of puppies through neglect? Why me and not someone talking young men and women into being suicide bombers? Why me and not dishonest oil executives? I knew it was a childish way to view cancer, yet it was what kept toddling across the screen.

Eventually the questions ganged up on me and attacked with the might of thousands: I was a victim of my own mistakes, my need for approval, my ego, my disbelief in myself. I floated all these thoughts lying in bed one night, the rest of my family blissfully asleep. I told myself that I was a health felon being punished for Cheeto-eating and not taking good care of this temple of the body. I hadn't exercised enough. I harbored too many negative thoughts. I ate my kids' leftover chicken nuggets and fries. I grew up in New Jersey. I had been way too judgmental about others, especially people who shared my flaws. I had not given enough of myself to my kids. No wonder I had cancer.

"Nobody gives themselves cancer." Nancy, who had survived colon cancer six years before, told me this one day over lunch at our favorite Mediterranean restaurant. "Think about how some children are actually born with cancer. How much more innocent can you get?"

I dipped my pita bread into some hummus and nodded. But the gnawing feeling persisted that if I had just lived differently, eaten differently, thought differently, I'd be healthy. I thought of people who smoked and then got lung cancer, people I would assume caused their own disease. Where does the blame end?

Within days I was doing what I usually do when faced with anything new: I headed to the bookstore, and after moseying on through a long list of foods I found in a book on preventing cancer, started composing a list of all the ways I would fix my life. Of course, I would eat right, figuring that if I could ingest enough squash, cabbage, beans, barley, figs, garlic, ginger, olive oil, orange peel, seaweed, soybeans, spinach, and turmeric each day I might be fine. Yoga regularly, along with meditation and prayer. Making collages that celebrated the healthy body. Avoiding caffeine, sugar, white flour, non-organic vegetables, red meat, and of course deep-fried fast foods. Herbs to build the immune system. Imagery to renovate my mind and clean out the dark cellars full of twisted perceptions. Of course I would lose the extra 30 pounds I was lugging around. All these things I could do if I was simply perfect each day.

I made list after list of how I would mend my ways. Sitting in our small greenhouse, I wrote in my journal how I would reform my life, save my body, be a better person. As if I had any control.

At Judy's house one day, she led me into her home office, a small, clean room with wood floors and a few well-appointed bookcases. We sat on the floor, and she handed me her best meditation beads. Judy sung to me the *Kwan Se Um* chant, the one asking the great mother for refuge. "It's a good thing to sing when you feel afraid," she said.

"Okay, I'll try it, but could you write it down for me?" She took a hot pink index card and starting writing the words and notes.

"You know, I tried to sound cheerful whenever I talked to you this last week," she told me, "but there were times I hung up, turned to whomever I having lunch with, and started crying."

Then she handed me the card.

I thought of my mother, how she became very quiet when I started reporting all the details. All the people close to me swimming through details too, downloading and uploading responses and realities. All of us waiting for what comes next.

Chapter Four:
The Impossible Gaze

The Torah portion at Saturday morning services was about Moses asking God to make himself visible. God told Moses that if he gazed at God's face, Moses would be dead instantly. As a consolation prize, God agreed to pass by as Moses ducked behind a rock so that Moses could glance at the back of God.

I sat in my seat in the small synagogue in the Jewish center, surrounded by a dozen or so congregants, including my son, whose Bar Mitzvah was speeding toward him like a bullet, and a few other teenagers in similar states of fear and boredom. I thought of the burning bush and this tiny ember of cancer burning in me. Something made of death, but then I supposed death was just another name for uncontrolled growth. Something alive but not life. A fire that could consume if left untended. I looked over at Daniel, trying to follow along in his prayer books in preparation for his upcoming Bar Mitzvah, but really, he was bored and tired. "Can we go to lunch afterwards?" he kept asking me, even though I kept saying yes.

"The Mad Greek?" he asked.

I nodded, but I was thinking of how we are made of stars, our hearts, with their complex machinery to uphold the rhythm, perhaps the center of the fire in the stars we're made of. I knew I hadn't been tending my heart as I should. Too busy chasing the heat outside me and now, this miniature burning bush in my left breast that I must tend, remove, let go elsewhere. Let it die down while I tend the fire of my life.

Over lunch, Daniel said he was angry at God for my cancer. It was a betrayal, he said, something that shouldn't happen.

"But it does happen. People get things like this all the time, and besides, what I have isn't so bad. It'll be over soon. Probably I'll just need this really easy kind of surgery, and then a little radiation."

"You're going to let them shoot you full of radiation?" he asked, his dark eyes shocked.

"Here, have more pita bread," I told him, turning away. He was angry, and to some extent, he was right.

That evening, Forest came to me when I was sitting in the greenhouse, reading a Goddard student packet on interfaith pastoral care for the dying. He was wearing his Harry Potter T-shirt backwards to hide the stains on the other side. His hair was sticking straight up in front, probably because of the bad hair cut I'd given him, and the double cowlick he had. "Mom, if they have to take those things," he said, shyly pointing to my breasts, "would you get something to wear under your shirt so it would look like you still have, you know...."

I told him yes.

A few days later, he asked, "Mom, is cancer like chicken pox that you can only get once?"

Each night, he gazed at me with that earnestness six-year-olds are made of. "Mom, how're you doing with the cancer today?" He was getting taller, almost up to my shoulders, and he tilted his head when he spoke sometimes.

Each time he looked straight into my eyes, face to face, his huge blue eyes waiting for mine, I could understand why Moses could only handle seeing God's back.

I visited Ursula every week, lying on the treatment table in the clean, white room of her house where she always had fresh flowers in a small vase on a table My eyes closed while she touched my toes, my hips, my shoulders, my head lightly; while she held her hands above me and around me, and I could feel the weather of myself calming. "Tell your body what's going to happen," she told me. "Prepare yourself for the surgery."

I began telling myself a story of what would happen as I lay still on the table, the birds outside loud in their leaps from branch to branch: Dr. Jew would cut my skin, and then lift out the globe of skin around the tumor— itself a small burning thing. Part of my breast. Part of what nurtured my children and brought them closer to me. I saw, further into the story: a teacher or guide would lift it up, carry it through the woods to a clearing. Prairie, rocks, desert. This guide would give it to the burning bush. The flesh would fall to the earth behind the bush, and be absorbed and recycled. The tiny ember of cancer in me would be transformed into a living sacred flame.

At subsequent sessions, Ursula led me through a guided meditation to envision my operating room, all the doctors and nurses and attendants, in a globe of light, and to also see myself traveling someplace safe for the duration of the surgery. While I've never been a beach girl, I saw the ocean, palm trees, sandy stretches, someplace tropical and warm, gentle and safe. I saw myself reclining on a giant palm leaf (hey, it was a visualization so anything was possible), and to my surprise, surrounded by a circle of women, all older than me, all tending me and giving me strength and love. Some had their hair wrapped in scarves, and looked as if they had been through it all and had strength enough to come back to tell the tale. While I didn't know it at the time, this circle of island women would come to me in quiet moments all the way through the cancer and beyond.

Ursula placed her hands on my shoulders, hips, feet, and forehead. I felt my body sinking slowly into itself, quieting, preparing. She encouraged me to tell my body what would happen, and I went through the story slowly, telling it to all my bones, all my organs, all my blood, and everything else that holds me alive.

The wild turkey showed up two weeks before surgery. It was during one morning after I spent a dizzying hour answering emails about the bioregional congress as fast as I could. I shut down the computer, and stepped out the front door one day, the air still chilled with winter's last breath, and there he was, less than 10 feet away. I looked at him. He looked at me. He had come toward the door from the side of the house, undoubtedly—as Ken would soon tell me—looking for a mate as all Toms do in early April.

He didn't turn his face and spread his feathers at me as he would have done with ease if I were a female turkey. He just cocked his head slightly, bowed as if he was going to call out, but stood silent.

When I returned late that afternoon, I walked quickly from the van toward the house while trying to drop my keys in my purse and answer my cell phone at once. I put my foot on the step leading up to the porch and paused, having already missed the phone call. The turkey was to my left, waiting. From then on, Mr. Turkey stood witness to my leaving each morning and returning each night, despite the other turkeys in our back field, over a dozen of them having the time of their lives together.

"A turkey is in love with me," I told Ken the night before surgery. Ken nodded as if it were perfectly logical, then put his hand over my left breast. We lay very still in the dark, both of us unable to sleep much, the heat from his body warming me and then overheating me. I kept obsessing about how I wasn't allowed to drink any fluids, and my obsession made me thirsty. We also had to wake up inhumanly early at 5 a.m., which of course made it hard to sleep.

"How is this going to be okay?" I asked him.

"I don't know. It just will be," he said right before falling asleep, something he was able to do like a famous magic trick, perfectly and quickly, while I struggled to get unconscious. He turned on his side, facing away from me, sleeping steadily.

In the "the witching hour," as Judy calls it, everything seemed worse. I reminded myself of this, but it wasn't enough to tidy up the mess of black, winding worries that clawed through me.

The next morning, of course, the turkey was there at dawn, standing guard as I got into the car. I waved to him and settled back into sleep for the drive.

After waking enough to enter the hospital with Ken and undertaking a small flurry of paperwork, I was taken by wheelchair to the mammogram waiting room, located below ground where the temperature is especially low. I knew they would have to put a wire into my breast leading toward the tumor, and then there would be the sentinel node biopsy prep, which I found out very soon I knew far too little about. Eventually, I was led to the mammogram room while another nurse explained to Ken that he couldn't stay there since it was a "woman-only" space. I was a little pissed off by this, but I had bigger fish to fry.

Ursula, who had been given permission by Dr. Jew to accompany me through all the pre-surgery procedures, was supposed to be here with me, but when I asked the nurse, a slim woman in Disney scrubs, about it, she brushed me off, too busy slinging my breast into the giant machine and moving the sides closer. When we were done, I sat back down, and she pulled out a black marker and a ruler. She applied them to the side of my breast, marking a place way up by my armpit where she thought the tumor was.

"That's too far away, it's down here," I explained, showing her a spot about four inches down. She shook her head, persisting in making marks near my armpit. Then she left to get the doctor to put the wire in while I worried that they were aiming for the wrong spot. I thought about a woman artist who made a poster of her naked torso before breast surgery with giant black lettering on one breast proclaiming, "Don't cut here."

Once alone in the room, I had a great urge to escape, especially since I thought Ursula might be stuck in the waiting room, so I opened the heavy door and started to sneak down the hall to get her. The hall was quiet at first, full of many closed doors. Then two nurses popped out, both adamant and one reeking of perfume, to order me back immediately.

"But my friend is supposed to be with me. She has permission from the doctor."

"You can't be out here. We'll ask the doctor about it."

A dapper man appeared soon, dressed in a suit, very relaxed and slightly cologned. "If it won't make her queasy, it's fine with me," he said. Then one of the nurses, the one whose perfume, combined with my fear, was starting to make me extremely nauseous, went to fetch Ursula. Meanwhile, the doctor studied my file and looked at where the nurse drew the bull's eye.

"The tumor is down here," he said, pointing to the spot I had tried to show the nurse. He drew a new bull's eye and by the time Ursula entered, squatted next to me, and held my right hand, he was ready to inject the long needle. Of course it hurt, but it was the type of pain that you can't remember afterwards, kind of like a miniature version of childbirth. With the wire now coming out of my breast, I had to undergo another set of mammograms, careful about smoothing down that wire before the machine made a run for my breast.

Once this procedure was over, I was led to nuclear radiology, told to lie on a narrow table that barely contained me, and left in the cold room with Ursula. In the dark room next to me, I saw flashes of light, and I could make out a woman lying on a table under a machine. I shivered, and Ursula put her hands on my shoulders and nodded. As soon as Mick, the technician, showed up, I asked him what was going on there. He explained that after the radioactive tracer was injected into my breast, I would lie under that machine until the tracer traveled to the sentinel node, kind of like magnets tracing each other. Suddenly, it didn't seem so bad to lie in the dark.

The doctor appeared again, this time with a pile of needles. He looked down into my eyes and explained that he had the distinction of having to plunge these needles into my breast. I was amazed and distraught that I had never asked anyone what a sentinel node biopsy entailed, and the sudden knowledge of this procedure's mechanics made me want to leap off the table and run toward the elevator. I couldn't understand why, in thinking about this, I never went to the response center in my brain to ask how the radioactive fluid would enter my breast.

It hurt. Actually, it was excruciating, and I started crying. While the needle diving into such a sensitive part of the body was bad, it was nothing compared to the burning ice feeling of the radioactive tracer making itself at home by racing down the ducts in my breast. I can't remember if there were four or five or six needles, only that I held Ursula's hand, and tried to envision golden light encompassing my increasingly-scared body. For years afterward, I heard from other women, including my own mother when she had breast cancer a second time, how this procedure wasn't painful for them. For me, it ranked right up there with the later stages of unmedicated childbirth.

Soon I was moved to the radiation room, where I lay on the table, balancing a Styrofoam cup taped on my breast to protect the wire hanging out. Mick explained that I probably would have to stay here for only 30 to 40 minutes, until the x-rays being taken would show the tracer riding down the ducts in my breast toward the pit stop of the lymph nodes. Some women needed to be here for two hours, and on rare occasions the procedure didn't work at all, but I needn't worry.

He was wrong. I was one of those rare women for whom the procedure just didn't take. For two hours I tried to breathe, surround myself with light, pray, relax. Periodically Mick would reappear, adjust the machine to take a shot from another angle, and then start the process again. Ursula sat in a chair across from me, wearing a pale blue shirt and vest, pale blue pants too. I could see she was concerned, and every so often I would hear her soft voice in her German accent, saying, "I don't understand what's happening here." Neither did I. While we couldn't talk during the procedure, I found out later that both of us felt like rabbits tossed into a penned yard of feral dogs.

The only reprieve came halfway through when my rabbi, a short and energetic woman who talked easily with her hands, showed up. I got to joke about how I had obviously increased a Styrofoam cup size while she held my hand and chanted the Misheberech.

Back in the dark again, as time went on, I got increasingly cold and nauseous. When Mick came to adjust the machine, I asked to him bring more blankets to cover my feet, and lift my dangling arm up and under the covers.

"Something is wrong," I told him. "The radiation is making me sick."

"That's impossible. It doesn't do that to people."

"But it is."

"No, it isn't. You're just reacting to other stuff."

Toward the end of my time there, I was shivering and became so faint that, for one of the few times in my life, I felt like I could pass out. Mick assured me it wasn't the radiation. But I didn't believe him, then or now.

Finally, Mick led me to a wheelchair, seeming a little pissed off that the pictures of my breast innards didn't show the tracer driving down the tracks to the armpit. Still, I needed to think about surgery, center stage, coming toward me quick now as I entered the prep room. Soon, my fear and loathing of the sentinel node biopsy were replaced with a roomful of friends wishing me well while Dr. Jew led in the surgical team. The nurses shook my hand, joked with me about the styro-breast, and told me their names. Within a few minutes, one of them asked me for my glasses, Ken took my wedding ring and put it in his pocket, and I was wheeled down the hall.

I don't remember arriving in the operating room or hoisting myself onto the table, although people later told me I was in great spirits. I don't remember the mask coming down over my face either. As in many movie scenes about the subject, the next thing I knew, I was coming to in the recovery room, finished with my first surgery. I managed to say that I was very nauseous, and that it hurt so much. I saw Ursula's face, tired and kind, and the face of a nurse, and I heard something about meds being injected into my IV.

Then I was moving, the ceiling of the halls morphing into the ceiling of the elevator, the padded walls of it coming into view, and then more white ceilings of long halls until we crossed a threshold to a small white square of a ceiling where I was transferred to a bed before collapsing asleep again.

When I woke, two things made it hard for me to get comfortable: the hateful machine that automatically took my blood pressure, squeezing my arm so hard I wanted to yell obscenities, and the fact that I didn't have my glasses and no one knew where they were. Without them, everything looked like a cross between art by Jackson Pollack and Monet, and the combination made me feel nauseous all over again.

"Maybe not being able to see clearly is an advantage," Ken said, putting something in the closet, perhaps my clothes that had disappeared so long ago, or maybe a stuffed giraffe by the shape of it.

"I don't think so. It makes me feel crazy," I told him, watching his tall figure shadow around the room while he talked with me like nothing much had happened.

Jerry came in, bringing me dried flowers from the prairie and listening gently as I ranted about the sentinel node biopsy, something that gave me rant material for a few weeks. Ken held my hand and asked if I was hungry, which I wasn't. Victoria and her husband Kurt dropped by to see how I was. My mother called, and Ken used the phone to call a small herd of people and assure them that I was fine.

The kids arrived with Courtney, Denise, and my glasses (which had made an unnecessary trip back to Lawrence in Ursula's pocket). Natalie handed me a beautiful picture of a Japanese anime character wishing me quick recovery. She was wearing a pink shirt with glitter on it, one of her favorite outfits at the time and one that I had bought her.

"How you doing, gorgeous?" Denise said, bending over to kiss me. She had a newly-shorn Mohawk, and in her short sleeves, I could see the Hindu goddess tattoo on one arm, almost smiling at me.

"Hey," said Courtney. She was smaller and slimmer than Denise, and usually dressed in dark, quiet colors and sturdy boots.

"It doesn't hurt much, and now it's all over," I said, without realizing that I was lying.

Natalie touched my arm tentatively, and Daniel stared at my blankets skeptically. Forest, looking sad, went to my other side and held my hand in his hand, nearly the size of my own. My breasts had been best friends to each of them during the two or three years that I nursed each of them, and I couldn't imagine how they would feel for them knowing there was cancer in their old food supply. There wasn't much to say, especially since I was so convinced that with this surgery the worst was over.

Daniel looked out the window, probably counting the cars in the lot, while Forest stood at the foot of the bed and looked down. They all seemed uncomfortable, their T-shirts too small or too large, their hair sticking out or just uncombed, looking as if they wanted to be far away from this bed and all the things they didn't understand.

"So how's the cancer going?" Forest asked.

"Hopefully, it's all gone," I said.

"It better be or I'm gonna beat its butt," Denise said, dissolving into giggles, which made Forest and Natalie laugh too. But Daniel just shook his head at us and tried—I could see in how tightly he held his lips shut—not to show the Technicolor rage and fear playing out in his mind.

"You know, there's a cafeteria in this hospital with hamburgers. Big ones," I said. Ken picked up my cue and they all left for a meal, their faces lightening just a little.

Feeling better and like I had survived the worst, I decided to celebrate by calling "room service." I delighted in the reality that this hospital, totally evolved into the 21st century, offered a wide variety of foods; you could call anytime, and they would bring you whatever you wanted. I decided on the fillet of sole with several vegetables, a fruit salad, and a cookie—I mean, if you didn't get a cookie after having your breast cut into, then something was wrong with the universe. I was a little startled by how small my voice sounded when I tried to say my order into the phone.

"Sure, honey, we'll get that up to you right away." I thanked the kind voice at the other end of the phone, my own voice shaking and out of control. "It's just fine, sweetheart, you're going to be okay."

Suddenly the room was flooded with back light from the window, the clouds cleared, and a 1950s, triumphant God-like sky arranged itself with sun and dramatic slants of light leading down to the earth. I hung up the phone and watched. The sun was on fire, consuming itself as usual. I sat up and watched the orange fireball balancing on the horizon, and realized that the future itself was the impossible gaze.

Chapter Five:
The Facts of Life

The air was cool and damp on my face as I walked into the house, the sky behind me a mountain of spent thunderheads. Stepping across the threshold and heading toward my room, I was full of fatigue and relief. Soon, I would get the call that all was fine, and soon it would be just some radiation, if that. I stopped, and went back out. The turkey was gone, a good sign, I told myself.

But within a day, I woke from a dream of shoddy houses built close to our own, while right outside my window, wild pigs were eating the flowers. Waking and sleeping again, eating and going back to bed, doubts of a happy ending trailed into my thoughts.

Like many post-surgery cancer patients, I focused my attention on the phone. Waiting for it to cry out with pathology report news became my least-favorite, but necessary, pastime. Of course, I was sore and terrifically uncomfortable, with a drainage tube hanging off my side beneath piles of cotton stuffed into the giant sports bra Dr. Jew had me wear. I looked a little like a breast enlargement surgery gone bad, and I had a rash up and down my torso from an allergy to the antibiotic. Soon, I imagined, Dr. Jew would call and tell me my lymph nodes were clear, and tomorrow I would call Dr. Stein to arrange to pop my ovaries out, the ending volley out of this nightmare.

Of course, the call didn't come all day as I mooned around the house with Ken, sleeping on and off, watching some movies, staring outside. So I anchored myself to the computer, preparing a press packet for the bioregional congress, and feeling some growing joy when I opened emails from other people focused on ecological work in Mexico and Australia. We had six months to bring this event together, and it seemed clear that all I needed to do was sit at this computer writing things and answering emails a little or a lot each day, and all would be well, at least with this part of my life.

When the call did come, I was home alone, Ken having gone to pick up the kids from school. I was so excited that I walked out onto our front stoop to hear my surgeon's voice clearly on the other end. The air was vibrant with spring, bird song, and light breezes. Dr. Jew sounded positive but soon said something about good news and bad news. I paced back and forth on the tiny deck, walking increasingly faster.

"The tumor was very small, only eight millimeters. We took out 19 of your lymph nodes, and the great news is that 17 of them are clear. Only two are involved."

Involved. She talked about this in some detail, but all I heard was that two lymph nodes had cancer. It was out of the chute. Chemo was no longer an option, but an inevitability. I was no longer stage one, easy and predictable, the path my mom and aunt took. Instead I was in another land where I didn't know the way.

"Oh my god, that's terrible!" Remembering my dream, I saw earth movers ripping up the ground around me.

"No, it isn't. It's great news. Seventeen of them are clear. Think of it."

"No, it's awful." I was starting to shake, my stomach trembling as I paced back and forth. That old terror of the stomach trying to leave the body. That old terror of something dark and filmy filling my lungs. I held the phone next to my crying face.

"Look," she said, "it's just a fact of life now. It's just like I'm Chinese and I have a small nose, and I'm going to be Chinese with a small nose the rest of my life. You have breast cancer and two lymph nodes are involved, and that's just the way it is, but it's going to be fine," she added with great cheer.

"How can it be fine? How am I going to get through this?" I managed to squeak out.

"We're going to pull you up by your bootstraps, and you're going to get through this just fine. Think of all the lymph nodes not involved." I listened to her and couldn't decide if it was good or bad to have such an optimistic surgeon. But then I realized that she saw people all the time who were stage three, stage four, people she had to notify that the cancer had metastasized to their lungs and bones, people facing issues labeled "quality of life" to avoid the word "terminal."

We said goodbye, and I dialed Ursula, walking through the house to the back deck where I had ample room to pace. She picked up and listened as I tried to contain myself enough to convey the information. The kinetic weight of fear and despair surged through me so strongly that I couldn't see how I could function, live, breathe with all this. But talking to Ursula, and later to Judy, Victoria, my mom, and Ken, I managed to sand off the edges of this pain by repeating the words. Nineteen lymph nodes. Seventeen clear. Two involved.

The news flashed across my brain like ticker tape. Nothing I could do anything about, yet it kept coming. I stood outside staring at the cottonwood tree in the garden, its teenage leaves emerging a little more fully and lately with more daring. How was I going to stand, sit, lie down with this?

I dialed Margo, my boss at Goddard, and told her the news. Immediately, she made plans to help shift a few students from me to other faculty, to give me more time and less work. "You're going to get through this great, kiddo. You're going as well as anyone could do," she reassured me. I tried not to choke up as I said goodbye to her.

Natalie walked into my room. "Can we have pizza for dinner?" she asked. She was carrying something, a piece of paper. Her hair was going different directions, and she was wearing jeans with sparkling red dress shoes. She looked afraid, but she also held the paper behind her back.

"Sure," I answered, trying to sound like a normal mom. "Go get one out of the freezer."

"Cool! Mom, you're the best," and then she sidled up to me, the T-shirt of stars glimmering with sparkles, and handed me the drawing she had just done of a can of soda filled with some kind of substance that makes breast cancer disappear. I stared at the green and yellow on the page long enough to stop shaking. She called the new drink she invented "the cure."

I looked up at Ken, who was walking into the bedroom behind her, and when she shot off to the freezer, I signaled for him to the close the door. He listened, looking as stunned as I felt. It seemed like I wasn't all there, but perhaps out on the other side of the world, terrified at all the soldiers in the Mongolian army.

"Well, what do you want for dinner?"

"Nothing."

"You've got to have something."

I thought for a moment. What does a person eat at a moment like this? "Mashed potatoes. With real butter." Dessert, that would be good too. "And raw cookie dough."

I never got through a chemistry class in high school or college. Something about the symbols, the jumble of letters, the precision needed for experiments when I was the kind of person who couldn't even follow a recipe without improvising always did me in. Yet "better living through chemistry" was my future. Chemo would start as soon as I had recovered enough from the surgery, and all of it would need to be balanced by an artful blend of medications.

The appointment with Dr. Stein was early Monday morning, after we spent only a few minutes in the waiting room with the angular fish tank that held a blue and yellow striped fish, a big white angel one, and something metallic green and fast. Once in the conference room with Dr. Stein, I had my notebook ready and my mind prepared to hear the inevitable. According to hearsay, I would likely receive four rounds of FAC followed by four rounds of Taxol. It would be months of agony, my life vacuumed out of me, my hair falling off in hunks, my eyes tired and confused, and I would go through menopause immediately (as if mood swings were needed on top of all this).

Dr. Stein sat down quickly, and handed us a piece of paper with some graphs on it. "Without chemo, ladies your age who are stage two have a 40% survival rate over five years," he said, pointing to the graph. I gulped. Then he pointed to the other graph, "And with chemo, it's up to 53%."

He went on to explain that this number included death from all causes, but all I heard was that I had a fifty-fifty chance of making it past the next five years. All this time, I'd thought I was barely tangoing with cancer, that my survival rate, if it were a grade, would be an A^+. Now it turned out that I'm failing the class. A nurse popped in and called Dr. Stein to help with someone for a moment, and he touched my shoulder as he left, said he'd be back as soon as possible.

Once alone, Ken and I stared at the charts, both of us completely freaked out by this news. "Why would he start with that?" I asked Ken later when we were driving home.

"Probably that's the protocol that they all have to start with."

For months afterward, when anyone asked me, as tons of people did, "What's your prognosis?" I thought of this moment, and I thought of how outrageously insensitive the question was, a question that basically asked if this cancer was going to kill me, and if so, how fast. I told hardly anyone what the graphs spelled out. It was difficult enough to tell my mother and hear her go silent across the hundreds of miles between her phone and mine.

Dr. Stein returned, and I immediately blurted out that I threw up easily and got nauseous at high altitude, or low-grade virus, so how could we handle this? He listened carefully and started describing drugs that would help me.

"Chemo isn't like it was 10 years ago. We have all kinds of ways now of controlling the nausea and helping people get through this." He leaned forward on the table and looked into my eyes, nodded a little, and then began.

There would be six rounds of FAC every three weeks. I felt a little shaft of joy: six rounds, not eight, and no Taxol. He handed me a study and went on to show me the lab reports of the tumor, and explain it all to me. He and Ken exchanged a lot of quick talk using terms foreign to me. He gave me copies of letters from all my other doctors about my condition and my, well, life. I wrote notes furiously, trying to contain things like how many blood tests, what danger signs, why mouth sores, when the rounds take place.

"We want you to continue living your life as best you can. And we'll do everything we can to make sure that you're okay. But keep in mind that we're treating this cancer very aggressively, missy."

"Where did you grow up?" I asked.

"Mostly Texas, but I was an army brat."

A man from all over, but he was right here, giving me every detail, listening intently, herding in pharmacists, nurses and anyone else to fill in any blanks. It was clear I would be supported here, surrounded by a group in constant contact with each other as the chemicals were poured into me. Ken and I filled pages with details and walked out two hours later, balancing handouts and fears, still stunned by the statistics with the sweet breeze of spring all around us.

That night, we called the kids to the table again.

"Now what? I can't take anymore," Natalie said, sitting down abruptly. "First the accident, now this cancer. If this is bad, I'm gonna sue!" Her voice was cracking.

"It's not that bad, I'm going to be okay," I said, hiding the tremble in my own voice, I hoped. "It's just that I need to have something called chemotherapy, and it's... ."

"Not chemotherapy!" cried Daniel. "You'll be throwing up all the time, and this means the cancer is still there, they didn't get it all. I read about someone who threw up her esophagus." I looked at him, suddenly realizing I needed to cut his hair which had grown past his neck and made him look more like a Danielle. His pants were also too short.

"Well, actually, they did get all of the tumor," said Ken, hedging a bit around the gory details, "it's just that there might be some cells left that could be a little bit cancerous, and it's important to kill them with chemotherapy before they go anywhere and... ."

"So why do you need to do chemo then? It's a terrible idea, and you shouldn't do it," said Daniel.

Forest was sitting very still, like he understood but couldn't say anything about it.

"The chemo is to kill any tiny cancer cells so that they don't turn into cancer," I said.

"But if they're tiny cancer cells, then they are cancer already," said Daniel.

"Well, maybe, but they're really small, like microscopic. The chemo is to make sure they don't develop into a tumor and go…" I stopped myself. How could I teach my kids what metastasis meant without freaking them out more?

"I've got a headache," I said, standing quickly, and rushing to the bedroom. I heard Natalie go to her room, slam her door, and start crying, then Ken going in after her to talk about it, Forest walking downstairs to play computer games, Daniel too. I sat up and took some aspirin, trying to imagine how I could still be myself while on chemo, and if not me, then who?

All through my cancer treatment, it was the little things that repeatedly hurt and surprised me the most—first the sentinel node biopsy, and now the port-installation, a seemingly kind and gentle minor surgery to pop a plastic port into my clavicle. Because I hadn't expected much pain, or even much time at the hospital, Ken went to work that day and my father-in-law, Gene, drove me to the hospital. Having this handy port would make it easy for my caregivers to plug in the chemo and at the same time avoid damaging my veins and possibly spilling and causing a chemical dump site on my body. I planned to be home in a few hours, watching some funny, stupid movies, and eating chocolate pudding to console myself.

On the way into town, I told Gene exactly what all the doctors had said. He nodded, not having known much cancer in his family but having experienced plenty of other illnesses and ailments himself over the years. He was a gentle man who had worked as a printing teacher at the high school. Back in the day, this assignment meant that he ended up with all the kids who today would be labeled "special needs." He liked to go shopping, driving all over town to get bananas on sale at one store, milk from another. Whenever I asked him how he was, he would give me his standard answer, "old and decrepit," but he kept running on some kind of secret source of energy and kindness.

We talked about the traffic, the new parking lot at the hospital, the way the volunteers even parked your car for you now. "Real service," he said, laughing a little, a man who had probably never encountered valet parking before.

While the parking went smoothly, the installation didn't.

The first mishap came when I had an allergic reaction to the antibiotic, adding another to the already sizable list of ones I couldn't take without breaking into hives. The nurse was great though, someone who knew all about the Highway 59 project, and she wanted to dish about the state highway department while I slowly recovered from the attack.

The second mishap was more general: a lot of waiting. This two-hour procedure took more like five hours, and there were lots of long gaps I filled by reading cake decorating tips while sitting in a fake leather, hospital scrubbed, easy chair in my thin cotton gown. A reprieve came when another nurse, a friend who also had breast cancer, dropped by to visit. She told me the size of her tumor, the chemo she was doing, the plan for radiation and more surgery, and she even showed me the fuzzy strands of hair still remaining under the colorful chef's style hat she wore at the hospital. She was able to function pretty well, and it was reassuring to talk with her, compare notes, doctors, and protocols.

The third mishap occurred as I was coming out of the partial anesthesia, which had actually put me all the way under. I threw up everywhere, and my friend, who had heroically shared her big, hard story with cancer, had to clean up the mess while I feebly apologized.

Finally, back in Gene's luxury car, driving all-too-slowly home, I discovered the fourth mishap: I was in incredible pain. My neck muscles spasmed, my head ached, my skin hurt where the port wires went down into my clavicle. In my clavicle itself there was a quarter-sized, hard plastic thing I couldn't stop thumping for weeks, thinking I would never, in a million years, get used to it. (I was wrong—it took only a few months.)

The painkillers made me throw up, which hurt my neck more. I ended up spending the night with rolled up towels under my neck, wet washcloths over my eyes to help soothe my migraine, the pain jolting me out of one disturbing dream after another. I heard the kids come in with Ken, argue with each other over dinner, race around the living room, go downstairs, come back up and eventually go to bed. But it was as if someone else's family, someone else's life had spilled out in this house where I lay like an invalid.

Over and over I would discover this ironic truth: it was the little procedures, the ones I never bothered to find out about or that I didn't think would be much trouble, that were the worst.

Days later, as I waited in Dr. Jew's well-appointed waiting room reading yet more magazines on decorating, I couldn't stop worrying. The lamp shone just so on my magazine, now lying open to an article on how to cleverly create better storage in your home office. I couldn't read it; I was more focused on whether the chemo would permanently harm me, and how it was that something so poisonous would help me. For days, all I knew was that I knew nothing, not even how I would feel hour by hour, when the terror might come and kidnap me onto a road trip of despair and concern, when the calm that all would be okay would unfurl in my being, when I would be able to sleep or eat. Normal life seemed like a fictional entity when there was a toxic site in my body. What exactly did I house and carry?

Outside the cottonwoods shimmered. A forest of them gathered on the banks of the creek near the hospital, dotting the garden, and lining the many roads between the hospital and our house where their leaves still glowed with the first flush of maturity.

I closed my eyes while I sat in the waiting room, and imaged the chemo as a dark forest I would have to cross beyond the actual cottonwoods, mostly at night, with occasional moonlight, starlight. Sudden clearings. Bramble. Unclear where the trails lay.

On the other side of this dark forest was the prairie and autumn with bright lanterns leading me toward them. The congress would be at the other end, just at the end of the last session of chemo, a kind of ritual to return to normal life. Although I didn't know the way yet, I could see the lanterns held by my family, friends, the people I loved. I thought of Ken, Victoria, Judy, Jerry, and other friends. I saw Ursula through the trees, alone but looking over at me, accompanying me from just beyond the path. I thought of my kids, my father and how confused he sounded about the chemo, and the warmth of my mother's voice when she said, "You take care of yourself."

I turned the page and encountered a woman modeling the essential jacket for spring, a boxy black linen thing. I closed the magazine and silently asked for the courage and strength to welcome all medicine with gratitude for its visits, to see each procedure and infusion as a guest helping me become more whole. To accept, breathe in and bless, release, and replenish myself.

The door opened and a bald woman about my age came in and sat down. She wore a kind of safari outfit, khaki pants with a matching jacket that tied at the waist, but what really drew me was her bald head, round and lovely. I tried not to stare at her, but I wanted to jump out of my seat and rush to her side, telling her I was joining her team. Instead the nurse called my name, and Ken and I put down our magazines and headed toward the small room where Dr. Jew gently pulled out my tubes, and told me I was healing.

We emerged and drove home, following the cottonwoods back to our own grove. The trees reminded me of the dark forest closing in around me each day as I woke up, anticipating all the nausea, headaches, and fear I could imagine the chemo bringing.

Meanwhile, other lantern-holders in my life began to gather. Emails arrived from faculty and students from Goddard College, some of them writing weekly to offer prayers and wishes. Juan, a student immersed in the Romantic poets of the 1800s while living in Puerto Rico and working for his father's furniture business, sent me yellow roses. Lee, an artist and former writing workshop student, now living in New Mexico with the next love of her life, mailed a get-well card at least every other week for months.

A lot of people asked to help—old acquaintances, members of the Jewish center, the highway group, even my exercise class. So we needed a plan. One night, a group of us sat down on the couches, mostly scavenged from alleyways and friends leaving town, Laurie with a note pad on her

60

lap. Kelly, a writer from the Highway 59 group; Laurie, an old friend I'd bonded with after her husband died; Barb, whose kids attended the same elementary school as mine.

"Okay, now you were saying you could be food coordinator for the first half of chemo, but not after that because you'll be out of town?" Laurie asked.

Barb nodded and said it was no problem. She and her husband Joe were wickedly-funny people who made wry remarks about the surreal musical performances at the elementary school. Like me, Barb wrote and taught, and we would frequently make fun of the academic life together.

We filled two couches, everyone taking notes but me. I tried to think of how to thank them, but anything I might say seemed inadequate in the face of what they were doing.

"I'm happy to take over after that," said Kelly, brushing her curls out of her face and pushing her glasses up on the bridge of her nose.

Laurie would be my press secretary, alerting people to anything we needed. Judy would continue being my personal attaché when it came to doctor visits and hospital trips. I handed Barb the email and phone list of people who wanted to help. We agreed on four meals a week, with an emphasis on fruits and vegetables and not too much dessert, or that was all that my family, in our weakened state, would ever eat.

"You don't worry about anything," Barb said a few days later as she brought the first batch of food over, much of it hand-baked or cooked by her. She brushed her dark hair out of her face and lifted containers and jars out of a large cooler. "People love helping." I remembered how, when Forest was just home from the car accident, she dropped by, listened to the details of what happened, and then burst out crying at our kitchen table.

She was right: in addition to the food deliveries formally coordinated by Barb and Kelly, food freelancers outside the loop regularly dropped off food. The refrigerator turned into a giant party host, holding plastic containers full of quiet potato soups, glass trays of chicken legs marinated in happy sauce, plastic-wrapped bowls of dozing mashed potatoes, occasional foil trays of ecstatic brownies. Every time I opened the fridge, I was greeted by the time, the energy, and the handiwork of my friends—all of which sheltered me wherever I walked, like a bright green spread of swaying trees.

The forest was dark and wide, trees everywhere, but there were also trees of life, and they bore amazing fruit.

Chapter Six: Chemopause

Short-Lived Greatness

I walked toward the Lawrence Memorial Hospital's automatic doors with Ken on one side of me, Ursula on the other, and a cloth bag full of snacks and juices, a good book, and my nerves. It was the first day of chemo, and I was nervous, edgy, and would have rather stayed in bed until I was brave enough do something far less daring, like watch a stack of stupid, funny movies and eat cheesecake. As we rounded the corner near the oncology center, I noticed a slight mix of disinfectant and new carpeting that smelled like chemo, or maybe pure fear, to me.

The nurse assigned to me that day wore a jungle print scrub and had slightly spiked reddish hair and a husband who had undergone cancer treatment himself. She immediately told me the details of each procedure that was heading toward me. She was just angular enough, and I was just tense enough that I almost started arguing with her for no reason.

She left to get the chemo, which somehow took over an hour to arrive from the hospital pharmacy, two doors down. "You okay with this?" Ken asked, his hand on my arm, and his face quiet. I nodded. I wasn't okay with this though; I was terrified about how my body would react. Ursula arrived, patted my leg, and sat down quickly. Judy followed, sitting on a stool, and looking into my eyes to see how I felt. She was wearing hot pink, which seemed somehow appropriate.

By the time the jungle print nurse returned, Ursula had to leave for an appointment, so, following Ursula's instructions, we asked the nurse if we could hold the chemo and bless it first on our own. She said of course, but she would have to stay there because it was a toxic substance. (On subsequent visits, we would be entrusted with the chemo alone and on our own, but not this time.) Ken, Judy, and I passed around each plastic bag of red or clear liquid, each diamond- or round-shaped pill, cupping each in our hands and uttering silent prayers. I watched how the others, one at a time, held the chemo, closed their eyes, bowed just a little, and nodded in tune with their thoughts and wishes.

As I held each item, I silently asked my body to welcome it, take it in fully, and then release it fully. I blessed it, and asked it to bless me, sort of like what Jacob demanded of the angels he wrestled with before he would release them.

From there it was an hour and a half of various things being infused into me—soft plastic bags the size of a hand filled with various poisons: the Kool-Aid-colored Adriamycin (doxorubicin), the clear Cytoxan (cyclophosphamid), the quick 5-Fu (fluorouracil), always proceeded by a host of little pills, syringes of steroids—balances and counter-balances. Throughout it all, I drank a wading pool's amount of water, which also meant that I shepherded my IV back and forth to the bathroom at regular intervals. I also ate an apple and some sesame sticks, trying to keep up my energy. Overall, though, I felt good, and on my way out I told Dr. Stein and some nurses that I felt great.

Short-lived greatness, but greatness nonetheless. By the time we got home, I started to feel terrible, shaky all over and engrossed by a high-speed headache. I picked up the phone, and dialed Ursula's number.

"I feel terrible. I'm going out of my mind."

"Do you want me to come over? I can bring the portable massage table."

"Can you?" She did, and within an hour, I was lying on that massage table between the bed and chair in my small bedroom, while she placed her hands on me.

"Look for an image, something that can help you," she said while I tried to bat away the rush of fear and exhaustion and hyperdrive inside my brain.

She urged me to connect with a star that especially spoke to me at some level. Years ago I had learned of a star named Carina, a sound very close to my name, so I placed myself somewhere in Africa, in the southern hemisphere where Carina shone. I felt the star above me, its light reaching down to my heart. I saw myself surrounded by the spirits I'd encountered during my first visualization sessions with Ursula, the "women of the island."

I woke up exhausted that night and for several nights to come. In the distance, I heard Natalie tell Daniel, "You've got to be quiet. Mom needs her sleep." Her voice seemed higher-pitched and edgier than usual. The two of them sounded like cats with scratchy throats, meowing at each other.

The truth was, I needed more than sleep. My kidneys hurt. I was constipated to the point of having powerhouse cramps, and I felt dazed. Dr. Stein advised drinking massive amounts of water, so I did, but I also slowed down too. As for eating, I suddenly understood the allure of pudding cups, which were quite tasty between watching movies, or answering more emails for the congress.

A few days later at Ursula's for a treatment, I felt such sorrow as she worked on me, as if the vitality of my body was being drained, and I was sad to see it go. I cried a little, and breathed deeply, trying to acknowledge the grief of being weaker. I also told my body that I was totally here with it, I would not abandon it during this time because we were in this together for the long haul. Maybe we weren't great at the moment, but we weren't leaving one another.

Buzz Cut

Debbie, my hairdresser for two decades, stood behind my chair in the beauty salon, looking at my overgrown and lopsided hair. She was wearing her usual mini skirt, slinky top, long blonde ponytail, and expertly-applied make-up. She put her hands on my shoulders, and started crying. "You can feel whatever you feel," she told me. "What you feel is just fine." We had spent years talking about our kids, her four husbands, the weather, the general state of the economy, and all the holes and gaps in the public school system

"Okay, I'll feel whatever I feel," I promised her.

She started snipping all around my head, and soon brought out the electric buzzer. I leaned back, relaxed. I would not have to worry about bad hair days for a long, long time. But what would I look like? Would my head be funny-shaped? Would I freak out every time I looked in the mirror? "Are you feeling whatever you're feeling?" she asked, her voice higher pitched than usual.

"Yes, I'm feeling whatever I'm feeling, and it's okay … I think."

Debbie buzzed and buzzed, trying to keep quiet. As my hair fell to the floor in greater and greater amounts, she finally burst out, "This is more traumatic for me than you."

When she was done, she wheeled me around and handed me my glasses like always. I looked carefully in the mirror.

"You have a wonderful round head," she told me, the first of what seemed like hundreds of people to say so. "It looks great on you."

I nodded, but all I could think when I saw my reflection was, "Holocaust victim."

At the end, I laughed a lot in nervousness and relief. This was me now—not rumpled but sleek, maybe hip. I pulled out my checkbook.

"No," she said, tears starting to fall from her eyes. "This one's on me." I hugged her goodbye as she cried into my shoulder.

Once home, the kids flooded me, leaping all over me to pet my head. They immediately renamed me "Puppy Head" and took turns coming up to stroke the soft black fuzz of my hair.

That afternoon, Forest and I walked to the deck together with a little plastic bag full of my hair, all swept up and bagged nicely by Debbie.

"We're going to give it to the birds so they can make nests out of it," I told him, both of us imagining baby birds sleeping in my hair, high up in trees. We each took handfuls, preparing to toss it all over the yard. I was amazed by how much gray there was in my dark hair as soft, weightless handfuls of it filled my open palms.

He was a little hesitant to take the hair, so I dropped some into his large, warm palm. He nodded and looked at me, waiting to follow my lead.

We leaned over the deck railing as I dropped finger pinches of hair on the emerging blanket of flowers, on the grass, on the bare spots in the dirt. He did the same.

"For you, birds, to make your nest," I said.

"Here, little birds, here is your nest," Forest called.

"Here, birdies, come get your building supplies," I added.

That night, as I snuggled in my bed under an old quilt while my mind spun a little too fast, reeling with an aggravating combination of utter exhaustion and leap-up-and-clean-a-closet restlessness, Natalie came in and petted my head softly.

"Oh, Puppy Head, Puppy Head, sleep well," she said.

James Bond, Meet Emily Dickinson

When the dexamethasone—a steroid I took right after chemo treatments to diminish nausea—took over, I could do anything. So I met Laurie, who walked or biked everywhere, to see if she was up for some movement. Very soon, we were taking a two-hour walk through the stand of walnut trees where she and her husband had married one fall day three years before he died of a heart irregularity, and through the nearby neighborhood. It was hot. Earlier in the day, we had walked past the lovely Victorian homes of Old West Lawrence, ending our stroll at Weaver's department store where we each bought ourselves a new dress—hers black and flowing, mine a sleeveless pink and green shift. We decided we looked splendid in these dresses.

By evening, I had answered several screens' worth of emails about the bioregional congress, sending people press packets for their local newspapers. I also talked high-speed with Ken about the Highway 59 group's plans for a shadow Environmental Impact Statement. We would research for ourselves the locations of endangered prairie flowers, Native American sites, and pristine woodlands, and tally up the safety statistics. Then we would present our data to the press and to the highway department, making our case that the present highway should merely be expanded instead of replaced with a new freeway.

That evening, I had also weeded an enormous vegetable plot littered with last year's remains, and put in an entirely new vegetable garden, not to mention the three rose bushes, some basil, impatiens, and other plants. All this after preparing a delicately delicious dinner, washing the dishes, sweeping the floor while singing show tunes, and talking profusely to all three of my cats. I was on a mission, and I couldn't believe the good fortune of having so much energy.

"Ken, isn't this incredible? I feel like I can get so much done."

He picked up his briefcase. Guaranteed for life when he got it 12 years ago, it now had wires springing from its worn edges. He was looking for something in it. "Uh huh."

"Years ago, back in college, I never did speed when other people did. I thought I would explode or something, but this is really great, and it suits me just fine."

He looked cross-eyed at me.

"I mean, if I have to be on chemo, I might as well get all this stuff done so that it's not a complete waste of time. You know, I was thinking of painting the hallway, maybe a pale color, and then I thought I should probably reorganize the linen closet first, you know what a mess that is." He walked into the other room, barely acknowledging my monologue about tidiness and renovation.

Earlier that evening, I confided in Jerry, who'd dropped by to visit and was immediately recruited to help me hoe the backyard, that Ken seemed a little depressed. "Well, considering he's living with a woman on steroids...." Jerry responded. He smiled at me, and continued hoeing.

Late at night, I settled into a two-hour project, planning a great vacation to Colorado—small cabin in an aspen grove, just 30 minutes from Denver, cheap and rustic—only to spend another hour unraveling the possibility for the trip when reality hit. By summer, I would be in the middle of round five or so of chemo. Not a very wise move. Who knows how I'll be—or who I'll be—by then.

I ended up trying on various dresses I never wore, then lamenting the loss of my new *People* magazine before trying to sleep again, my mind filled with criticism of Pamela Anderson for entering into such a thoughtful marriage and having such big breast implants that surely her back was killing her. At 3:15 a.m., I was wide awake again, having just read a student's manuscript on the social history of the bra, and I was preparing a letter in response to it. I understood that I was zoned on the dex, and even after I took some sleeping pills, I was still zoned. So I surrendered to being hyper and tried to pretend this was mid-day, and I was at work.

I woke up at five the next morning after an hour of sleep. I watched Ken wake at six, sit up and look at me, puzzled. "I've never seen you up at this hour before me." I smiled, didn't even lift my hands off the laptop, and kept going. These steroids were great, especially for me, a person who couldn't even drink a cup of coffee without being up half the night. I felt like James Bond acing a secret mission, cleaning every closet, folding every pair of pants, and even finding time to answer three days of congress emails, send the press packet to another dozen publications, and make a color-coded chart for congress workshops.

But what goes up must come down. My luck, and the dex, ran out after my three-day high, and gravity won as it always does. A migraine hit my right temple with the force of Mike Tyson, and I had spasms in the muscles at the base of my skull too. I lay down with a wet towel over my eyes and downed twice the maximum allowable dosage of aspirin. I kept hearing one of my favorite Emily Dickinson poems in my head, "I felt a funeral in my brain." The pounding was wild, the exhaustion profound, and nothing brought peace.

Then chemo brain struck—something I can only compare to PMS on, well, steroids. I could barely make it to Ursula's, arriving for my appointment 30 minutes ahead of time so I could nap on her couch. I was exhausted, in pain, so diminished that I felt like most of my energy had been sucked out by a giant vacuum cleaner, or more accurately, a posse of secret agents looking under the bed and opening drawers, all seeking ways to damage, confuse or trick my dithering DNA.

If my organs could speak, they would yell in unison, "We're confused, we're confused, we're fabulously confused!" I told them to just hang on, that I was there with them through it all, and once we got through the first chemo round, we'd all know more about what was in store. They seemed skeptical, but it wasn't like they had anyplace else to go.

Healing Circle

Every place has its season, and Kansas did spring like nowhere else: the lilac-colored redbuds lit up the pale green of the woods, the fields turned green, the breezes lightened and floated like feathers falling down, and the sky grew large.

On one tender evening in May, Ken and I left the kids with their grandparents and headed out to Nancy and Jim's place for one of my healing circles, which thankfully met once each month. I had called together about a dozen beloved friends, many of them survivors of cancer or partnered to people with cancer. We got together so they could hold my hand, tell me funny stories, and hold in their hearts any bad news.

In truth, the idea for the healing circle came from the time several years ago when I was part of Nancy's circle, when she had cancer. It was such an honor to be part of the small group of family and friends who met with her every so often and sat in a circle around her to hold her and send prayers for healing.

In the driveway beside Nancy and Jim's house, south of town where wide fields stretched around us, we met Diane, a good friend who had lost her life partner to breast cancer. I waved to Jolene, another old friend who had survived colon cancer. Next, Jerry walked toward the house, and then Laurie, who had won me over for life when she told me, after the sudden death of her husband, "I'm in for the ride of my life." Anyone who could navigate grief with such openness was someone I wanted close to me.

The house was a large old bungalow, complete with a welcoming porch, that had been moved from town to the country years before Nancy and Jim arrived in Lawrence. Stepping in, I could smell the savory food in the oven, and as always, marveled at how clean, bright, and creative each cleft and counter was. Some held pine-needle circles around candles, and some were laden with orange and yellow bowls beside a flair of forks.

71

This night, Jim and Nancy gave me a healing box they made for me, purple with a collage of healing images. Each person in the circle then put something in the box: a doll who would take any negative experience and transform it into pure energy, a stone heart, some buffalo fur, a prehistoric tool made from a rock, a crazy plastic lizard woman with breasts, little stones, and a card from Laurie, telling me she had my new dress taken off my Weaver's charge card and put on her own. Afterwards, I lay down and they sat around me, each putting a hand on me to reassure my body that it was okay.

I let myself relax as much as I could, trying to absorb the love and energy from this group of people I loved fiercely in return. I tried to accept that it was okay, although I had the repeated urge to throw myself down and raise my arms up and down, crying out, "I'm not worthy," like the *Wayne's World* guys.

Other nights we spread ourselves out on Nancy and Jim's couch and big chairs and talked, mostly about cancer: how it was judged in this culture, the importance of being open and not being silenced by it, the ridiculousness of magazine articles that promoted the "cancer personality" (the person who gets cancer through repression), coping after chemo, the need for alternative support groups and practices to help recovery, and our favorite topic of all: the dumb things people say to people with cancer.

"Yeah, and he yelled out, in the middle of this Mexican restaurant, 'What's your prognosis?' Like I'm gonna tell him the percentages."

"I got that question a lot too," Jolene said, "and eventually, you know what I said? 'We're all going to die. I just don't know when.'"

"We're all gonna die!" people in the group yelled out, making us laugh harder.

"You wouldn't believe the questions I get at my job." Because Nancy was a nutritionist at our very busy food co-op, I could only imagine. "Like I was standing on this ladder, putting up a display one day, and someone comes to the bottom of the ladder, and yells up, 'What kind of cancer do you have?'"

We laughed harder, knowing that yelling down "colon cancer" would be outrageous.

"It gets worse," Jim said, putting his hands up. "People want to know how she got this cancer. I mean, she's so healthy, she's a nutritionist, she eats well and takes care of herself, so if she gets cancer, they start wondering about themselves."

"What did you tell them?" Ken asked.

"You could say you got it from anal sex, that would freak them out," someone said, and we laughed so hard that we started falling out of our chairs.

"Anal sex, now that's funny," said Jim.

"Just remember, we're all gonna die!" We laughed until it made my stomach ache during the drive home, down into the softly-cool valley and back around to our home.

Hospital Relay Race

I walked into my house, late for another weekly Highway 59 meeting, but my absence had not prevented a highly-energized roomful of people from letting themselves in. I was relieved to see that they were clearly at home here, even helping themselves to iced tea. Miriam, Almeda, Newton, Retta, Ozzie, Kelly, and Bruce sat on the floor, crawling over maps of potential routes and passing around documents they'd found.

"This is ludicrous," said Ozzie, shaking his head and rolling his eyes. "They expect us to believe this? Who are these guys that they think they can just lie to us and then ram the highway through?"

"It's how the big boys always operate," said Newton, a retired emergency room physician and history buff, adding quietly, "The bastards." He shook his head and stared at the floor. Newton lived smack-dab in the middle of the proposed new freeway route, in a stone house passed down through the generations to him.

"Well, what we need to do is figure out what we want to say in our response," said Kelly, who had her pen and pad out. An environmentalist who biked or rode public transit to avoid using her car, Kelly also had an eye for beautiful cats. "Caryn?"

I tried to sit with them, sinking to my knees and then settling onto the floor next to a map of the northeast Kansas corridor, but my head started swimming. Or rather, something distracting, a chill with a flame on the end of it, started swimming in my head. "Huh?"

"The introduction to our draft, what should we start with?"

"Well, if you ask me, we need to talk about the Reno road and its impact. It would just be a mess when there's heavy rain," said Almeda, a Republican farmer's wife and leader of the Farm Bureau who grew hollyhocks the height of basketball players. Almeda and her husband lived north of Ottawa, where their family homestead, generations under their feet, faced extinction if the freeway went through.

My head ached, my body shivered. I didn't know how to begin our letter, and actually, I didn't feel right being in a vertical position. I pulled myself to my feet and excused myself, went to the bedroom to take my temperature, while voices behind me were saying how chemo sucked...just like the highway department. If my temperature ever crept above 100 degrees, I was doomed to do a hospital run because the chemo, in the process of eradicating my immune system pill by pill and infusion by infusion, might have opened the floodgates for a deadly infection.

In our bedroom, I sat in my chair with a thermometer in my mouth, paging through an old *People* magazine and waiting. I could hear a man laughing and then a woman joining him, the melodic sounds rising to shrieks as others joined in. I heard Bruce say, "All right, people, calm down" as I pulled out the thermometer. It read 100.7, so I called the doctor, whose office confirmed that I needed to get to the hospital. I signaled Ken, who had started explaining a better proposed route for the highway. "The hospital," I told him in the hall, "I have a fever, we have to go."

"Okay," he said calmly, seemingly taking it all in stride, and turning to explain that we were leaving.

"You'll watch the kids, right?" I asked the group. All three kids were downstairs, enmeshed for the moment with the new VCR and television my mom sent to help me through chemo.

"Of course!" said Miriam. "Can we do anything else?"

"You okay?" Bruce, our lawyer, was concerned enough to look up from the piles of government regulations and highway maps. "You know, this cancer is absolutely uncalled for. It's completely unwarranted." If he could have sued someone for me, he would have.

"It's a sham," said Lori, a Lakota activist with long black hair down to her butt and a genius for legal research.

"I hate that you have this," said Kelly. "It makes me furious."

"Those bastards who ruin the environment, it's their fault you have cancer," someone else said.

"Sure," Ken said, "she'll be fine. Just finish the meeting, and take good care of our kids, okay?"

"You take good care of yourself," said Newton, the retired physician.

"We'll be thinking of you," said Miriam.

The time at the hospital was typical hospital time—suspended in slow, overly-cool, clean rooms with never enough good magazines. Ken talked about anything we could think of while people came and went, taking my blood pressure or blood, or escorting me down the hall for a chest x-ray. In the small emergency room where I put on a gown and was told to wait, I waded through a *Newsweek*, finding only movie reviews of the new Harry Potter film to hold my attention. We split a spongy granola bar from the candy machine, and I sipped a bottle of water. As usual, the room was chilled just enough to make it uncomfortable to wear a gown that left my legs and back exposed. Nurse Bill, a lanky fellow with one studded earring and a crew cut that matched his barely shaven face, stuck his head in every so often to check on us.

Finally, after my white blood cell count came back up to 1300, an indication that my blood was good and ready to fight off invaders again, and my temperature dropped, the doctor on duty reported that he had consulted with Dr. Stein. The game plan was a heavy antibiotic right now, plus a shot of neupogen—a drug to help raise my white blood cell count further—and homeward bound I'd be.

We got home at 1:30 a.m. to find a phone message waiting from Nurse Bill, informing us that he forgot to flush my port, so we'd have to come back in. I was so tired that I was starting to see double. Ken tried to talk me into going back; instead, I called Bill and asked him if it were possible for me to take care of it tomorrow when I visited the oncology office. Luckily, Bill reached Dr. Stein, and the plan flew.

The next day at the oncology center, I sat in the too-hard recliner with my feet up, my right arm connected to an IV. I tried nibbling on an energy bar to make up for hardly eating for two days. The dreaded mouth sores had moved in. I remembered the fire swamp scene in *The Princess Bride* when the princess and her beloved (also known as the latest Dread Pirate Roberts) battle quick-sinking sand, exploding trees, and R.O.U.S. (rodents of unusual size). What would be next for me?

Because of the fever, and the strong suspicion that an infection was camping out in my internal background, a separate IV stand was set up to pump in the antibiotic. Meanwhile, the gorgeously efficient team of nurses arranged for me to take intravenous antibiotics at home, too, with Ken administering them regularly.

That evening, while the kids watched more Japanese animé, a pair of women dropped by our house with IV equipment and drugs.

"I grew up here," said Sandy, "and I just love the prairie."

"Me too," I answered, "although I grew up in New Jersey. But I love the wide open sky."

"You have a good view here," she said, as we turned to the window to see the green in all directions, the hills around us like the perimeter of a large green bowl, the blue sky startling in its simplicity.

"Yeah, we can see the weather coming in," added Ken, who was sticking a frozen pizza in the oven for the kids, then returned to watch how Sandy would be giving me antibiotic.

"I like feeling like I live in the sky," I added.

"So do I," said Sandy. "Hey, you know what they say. 'There's no place like home,'"

"Thanks, Toto," I answered, and she laughed.

She was attaching a plastic sac of clear fluid to an IV pole, showing Ken how to insert it into another port, this one on the outside of my skin, attached to my right arm. She made us practice together. Four times a day for 10 days I would get this antibiotic, and it was unlike any antibiotic I had known before: it made me so exhausted that I spent much of that time lying in bed, staring at the ceiling, too tired to sit upright and too bored to go to sleep. Time slowed to the pace of waiting in the wrong line at a supermarket. There was nowhere to go.

In addition, my routine would now include Ken giving me shots of neupogen, a medicine that induced flu-like symptoms, for six days during the third week of each four-week chemo cycle.

After our routine of me pointing to a place on my outer thigh, then him sterilizing the spot with alcohol, filling the needle, and plunging it into the spot—sometimes it hardly hurt and sometimes it burned like crazy—we always had our standard joke afterwards: "Was it good for you?" Like most dark humor, it was a little bit true: the chemo, and the dread of death we were both going through, had seriously dampened our sex life.

He didn't laugh, just shook his head as he wrapped up the used needle for disposal. He was wearing red plaid pajama bottoms and a sleeveless T-shirt, and I was in a floaty pink nightgown that pleated over my breasts. The wind was up, a storm was approaching, and I shivered a little. Only years later would he tell me how much he hated sticking that needle in me each night.

This first night, though, as the visiting home health care people watched to make sure we did it right, Ken held the needle between his palms, silently blessing it. In the background, Daniel yelled at Natalie, "My sister, the politician," and she yelled back, "My brother, the jerk."

We were home.

"We must know each other," we kept saying, but we didn't. I was at the annual Relay for Life, held in the Haskell Indian Nations University stadium, standing opposite a woman who looked as completely familiar to me as I did to her. She was probably 20 or 30 years older and completely bald, just like me.

"It's like we were separated at birth," I told her while we touched our foreheads like cone heads greeting each other after a jaunt to Pluto and back. Of course, we were wearing the same purple T-shirt given free to all the cancer survivors.

She told me her name and that she was being treated the third time around for breast cancer. Her eyes were bright bluish-green, close to the color of my own eyes, and with her bald head and pale skin, she seemed all eyes. "The second time," she said, "the chemo didn't do anything. It didn't even touch the cancer." We hugged, joked like we'd been pals forever, and walked a lap together with other survivors.

What I didn't know was that she would be dead before the year was out. Months from this day, at a breast cancer support group, I would hear the story of how she told her grandson, just days before her death, that when he felt a breeze in the trees, it would be her. She would come from wherever she was then to tell him how much she loved him.

I knew that cancer was a relay race, but there was no way of knowing when it was your time to walk. There was only a big track with seemingly endless loops of the same kind of hope that people put into those votive lights in white paper bags, each one with someone's name on it.

The Tattooed Lady

I didn't hate my hair. Most women I knew did, or at least fought with their hair occasionally when they weren't banishing it to pony tails or short cuts. For me, my hair had been one of the few things right about my otherwise flawed appearance. When I hit puberty, my straight-as-a-pin thin brown hair suddenly turned curly and thick. I'm still not sure how it happened so quickly, but at the same time, my brown eyes turned hazel. All I knew was that one day, when I was 15 or so (I'd always been a late bloomer), I looked in the mirror and saw a girl with curly hair and green-brown eyes. I still lacked the freckles and high cheekbones I longed for, although my daughter ended up with those cheekbones through the magic of genetics.

I grew my hair long, I cut it short, I grew it out again, I permed it for extra curl in the winter when my hair tended to go flatter, and then cut it all off again on a whim one hot summer day. Still, it always came back, fast growing and so easy to maintain that I didn't own a comb or brush.

After my buzz cut, right after the second chemo treatment when my hair was supposed to fall out, it fell out in such slow motion that I started to look less like a Holocaust victim and more like a very confused duckling. That was when I called Courtney and Denise. Veterans of shaved heads, and lured also by the promise of spaghetti and meatballs, they came right over.

While the pasta boiled, Denise shaved a checkerboard on my head, telling me it looked awesome. Courtney nodded, but Ken, walking in the door after a long day at work, told me I looked like a gang member. The kids trailing behind him just gaped at me.

I went to the mirror. White supremacist. Not really my look. So I asked Denise to shave it all off.

Back at the mirror, with Denise's giggles behind me telling me I looked beautiful bald, I found an image of someone hairless but friendly. I decided that it was also a good summer cut, so to speak, given that my only other options were hats, do-rags, and wigs.

Bald. That's what I'll do, I thought at that moment looking in the mirror. At least, that was where I started out.

Sometime after spaghetti and meatballs, with Courtney and Denise joking about my cool new look, and talking about how Denise planned to get pregnant within the next year if they could just find a willing donor, I found my hand reaching for a pack of fake tattoos. Birds. All different kinds—cardinals, blue jays, eagles, owls. Some of the birds had wings outstretched, mid-flight, and others were perched or nested. The tattoos were Natalie's, and neither she nor I could remember where she got them.

Tattoos. Bald head. A flash of electricity jumped between them. I knew what I had to do.

I put a cardinal right over my left eye, a goose over my right, and the others became part of the garland around my head. Flight. Wings. Color. Beauty. They just seemed to belong there.

When I came back to the table, where Forest was passing out ice cream bars, he started giggling. "Are those permanent?" Daniel asked.

"Oh my god," said Natalie, but she was smiling. "Mom, you've got freaking birds on your head!"

Ken opened his mouth but didn't say anything. Denise applauded and rushed up to hug me. Courtney rolled her eyes.

The tattoos were indeed temporary, and within a week, my birds started to tatter, but I found a toy store that carried temporary tattoos. As word got out among my friends, tattoos started coming in the mail, including even some Frida Kahlo paintings. I never could figure out how to apply the large image of Frida's face.

It became a ritual: once a week, I would shave my head smooth of the nubs that had started to erupt, and then carefully, with a wet washcloth, apply a circle of mammals, amphibians, butterflies, or sometimes flowers. The ring of flora or fauna lightened up the chemo for the kids and me, and took the bald edge off my life. Once, as I lifted a bag of groceries, a woman called out, "Hey, I like your fishies."

I turned and looked at her, trying to smile as I said, "They're whales."

I walked into the hall of Forest's elementary school where some kindergartens stared at my head, so I bent down.

"Wow! Dogs," one said.

"That one looks like our puppy," said another.

For a chemo appointment, I wore flowers, small delicate pansies, daisies, and roses. For a taco dinner at Ken's parents' house, I sported small woodland creatures, a fox over my third eye. For getting the oil in the car changed, I wore wolves. I wore prairie dogs to a Highway 59 meeting, farm animals to a bioregional congress potluck.

One day, when a teacher saw my bald head as I picked Natalie up, he looked at my garland of galloping horses, and called out, "Hey, who did you lose a bet with?"

"God," I answered.

But it turned out that at least God had a good sense of humor, and there was something about wearing a ringlet of kittens around my scalp that made chemo seem a lot less like a pact with the devil.

The Target

I woke up in the middle of the night with searing bone pain all over. I swallowed some drugs, but it took a long time for me to fall back to sleep.

It seemed that my left side was especially hard-hit by the bone pain. It was a long, depressing day until I started cleaning house in the mid-afternoon and tidying the boys' room, which mainly consisted of making a pile for the socks that had obviously multiplied over time, another pile for old computer and *Mad* magazines, and a third pile for trash and orange peels.

Later that afternoon, I drove to Target to pick up something for dinner, my sadness and confusion traveling sidecar with the rest of me. The parking lot was full, and I circled around a row of cars to find a spot just opening up. After the S.U.V. pulled out, I glided the van in and, still tender in my depression, stepped out onto the hot pavement. A truck rolled close and a man with a square chin and a unibrow leaned out the window. "Hope you got what you want!" he yelled.

"What do you mean?" I asked.

"I was waiting for that spot."

"Oh, I didn't see you. Look, I can move."

"How could you not see me? I was right here." He screamed at me as if I were a total idiot, then pulled away quickly. I started shaking with a kind of rage that surprised me. Who was this guy and how could he think, given my state of mind, that I would steal a parking spot from him? My mind began obsessing about what had happened as I walked into the store. A minute or two later, I saw the same man heading toward house wares.

"Hey," I yelled as I approached him. "I didn't mean to take your spot. I just didn't see you."

"Oh, yes you did," he said.

I could see, up close, that he was just a fifty-ish guy, a little tired-looking and probably not all that vengeful, but I still felt the explosion of anger in me. How dare he accuse me of stealing a parking spot? I'm not that kind of person. As I tried to explain it to him, a continuous ticker tape ran through my mind, "Don't say 'fucking asshole,' don't say 'fucking asshole'...."

Too late. "Look, you stupid asshole," I shot back at him. I was wearing a thin baseball hat, but it should have been obvious that I was bald and not doing all that well. "I didn't mean to take anyone's spot, and I was willing to move and give it back to you so why don't you just...."

He leapt toward me, and for a moment I thought he was going to hit me. How crazy was I to have brought this onto myself? "Don't antagonize crazy people," Ken had told me for years, and here I had done it now with the verbal equivalent of a big exclamation point. But instead, the man leaned into me, and in a low whisper said, "You, you better get hold of yourself." Then he turned on his heels and walked away.

When God Makes a Mistake and Other Blessings

My mother entered the house flanked by her husband, Henry, and armloads of shopping bags. The kids crowded around, Pavlov's dogs by now in how well they understood that Grandma arriving meant gifts. She gave them T-shirts and toys, some books, the mandatory candy. The kids got the goods, then scattered to open plastic-encased video games and purple roller skates.

My mother, just 18 years older than me and my same height, wore a big-shoulder woodpecker red jacket with rhinestones trailing into vines and leaves of purple and blue. Henry, 20 years her senior but just as spry, tall with a hunched-over posture and a beautiful beak nose, nodded. As usual, he wore one of his many caps, this one forest green and sporting a logo for his son's engineering company. He was the love of her life, and she, the love of his.

Before my mother put down her bags, she pulled out one last gift, a small, purple-wrapped jewelry box. "And this is for you," she said.

Inside was a Chaim, the Jewish symbol of life, a talisman for luck for me to wear around my neck. I held the gold symbol in my palm. The perfect gift. I promised to wear it everyday until I was out of the woods.

No one in our family had done chemo before so it was a kind of dangerous delicacy, and everyone, although they didn't speak to me directly about it, was nervous about my cancer. In a way, it was similar to when I got the first graduate degree in the family, only there were never any arrogant professors to get angry at.

For two days, we got in the car and went: we had a Bar Mitzvah to outfit, and that meant flashing the debit card for plenty of paper plates, trays of smoked salmon, bags of bagels, giant challahs, napkins, liters of soda, and 20 giant pizzas. I was relieved that the week before, Natalie, Judy and I had driven to Kansas City to find a dress for me to wear. Now, with the steroids going full force, I was up for the moving part, but not the sitting still parts. Driving back from Kansas City one afternoon with our new carload of edibles, I looked at the little car clock.

"How can I sit in this car for 20 more minutes?" I asked no one in particular. "I'm going to go out of my mind, I feel so spaced out."

Daniel, in the backseat, a veteran of years of an unreliable attention span, said, "Oh, Mom, I know exactly how you feel." He was just on the verge, we would find out later, of slowly unfolding from a slightly-chubby, short, dark-haired boy into a pencil-thin man with high cheekbones and the kind of shoulders that Judy said would make him a perfect model for the button-down shirts he would wear only under severe pressure.

The night before the flood gates opened, bringing all the relatives from Pennsylvania, New Jersey, Manitoba, and Oklahoma, we had a garden-weeding party with friends, including one who'd had the poor luck to ask that day if there was anything, anything, she could do. We attacked the flower beds with a vengeance, pulling out weeds while I tried not to fantasize that they were cancer cells, an utterly defeating image because the weeds could obviously never be conquered.

The Mongolian army images weren't working for me either, making little sense the more I thought about them—I mean, did I actually want my body subjugated by Genghis Khan? I had read of someone who imagined animals eating the errant cells, but in the end, I never could settle on one compelling image of how the cancer would be defeated.

So I turned to ice cream, three kinds to set out on the counter. The weeders and I took our cups of cherry vanilla and chocolate swirl ice cream to the deck, watching as the dusk filled in the space between us and our good work.

The energy of the Bar Mitzvah on that Saturday morning propelled me onward, despite the fact that I had awakened in the middle of the night, and, while trying to take a pill to prevent vomiting, gagged and threw up all the way to the bathroom. Now, all dressed-up in the daylight, complete with fake jewel tattoos that I stuck all over my head, I zoomed around hugging people, many of whom told me I looked elegant although I thought I looked more like a Russian Orthodox Easter egg propped on a body.

My father (who had surprisingly lost some girth from his considerable stomach) and my stepmother had arrived the night before, as had my sisters, Jennifer and Lauren, Lauren's husband, Eddie, their kids, and Jen's fiancé, a quiet man named Eric. Never mind that Jen hadn't talked to my dad since a blow-out 13 years earlier, while Lauren hadn't spoken to him in the several years since they'd had a massive fight that ended with her throwing a phone, him still on the line, through a wall. It was par for the course in my family, and now, to have everyone together meant we were all just a little bit jittery, especially me, but then I could blame that on steroids.

The next day at the Jewish Community Center, most of the 200 chairs were filled with family and friends, whose circles overlapped in surprising ways. I saw some Highway 59 farm wives and their husbands walk in a little hesitantly, their first time at anything Jewish, but they were soon joking with a Lakota rabble-rouser and my tall (at least for our family) sister, whose daughter looked like a miniature version of Botticelli's paintings of full-lipped, curly-locked women. Organic farmers discussed the weather with seasoned New Yorkers. Poets, neighborhood organizers, lesbian couples who called each other "my wife", and academics hauling big babies found themselves sitting together.

When the service began, the first thing the rabbi did was to call my father to the bema so he could present his tallis to Daniel. Most Bar Mitzvahs typically begin with a relative giving the young person about to cross over the theoretical threshold of adulthood a tallis, a prayer shawl, along with a prayer. I got the shawl from my mother, who got it from my brother, who got it from my father, and I returned it to Dad, asking him to present it and any words he had to Daniel. But apparently Dad had left the tallis at his hotel and had gone to fetch it when he was called. Because Daniel had to wear something, another member of the congregation rushed up and covered him with his own oversized white tallis.

A few minutes later, after Dad returned, the rabbi called him up, and I watched my father put the prayer shawl, a small white one with blue trim and the customary fringes, around Daniel's shoulders.

"Do you want to say something?" the rabbi asked.

He paused, looked at Daniel, and said, "May you grow up to be a mensch." A mensch is Yiddish for a good, sound, ethical, and upright person. It was the best thing my father could have blessed Daniel with, and Ken and I smiled at each other. "A mensch," Victoria told me later, "that's what we all want to be."

After another hour of prayer, we arrived at the part where Bar Mitzvah kids and their parents make speeches, usually resulting in tears, hugs, and the throwing of candy. Ours was no exception.

Daniel spoke about a Torah passage that concerned Moses and the people of Israel wandering in the desert. At some point, the people got restless and started to wonder if they should have come, and an opposition leader to Moses emerged, asking why they had to follow such limiting rules. Moses and God consulted on this, and the next thing you knew, God opened up a huge pit in the ground and had it swallow up all the opposition. Don't mess with God. Don't mess with Moses. End of the story.

But for Daniel, it wasn't the end of the story, and his speech concerned how God should have listened to the opposition and looked at how everyone could reach consensus. Sometimes, he said, opposing viewpoints gave a person better perspective or stronger ideas. Daniel went on to say that while it might look like the earth opening up and swallowing the opposition was a miracle, it wasn't; it was just God making a mistake. A real miracle was when his brother, Forest, not only survived a terrible car accident, but healed without any long-term effects. Real miracles were made of healing, people helping, survival.

When it was my turn to speak, I told about the futility of all those child-rearing books I'd read before I had Daniel, how he always defied convention. A boy who felt so strongly about protecting others that he once threw himself into a pack of cub scouts who were tossing live insects into a campfire, Daniel's convictions and visions always guided him fully. Then Ken spoke about becoming a man, taking responsibility, and also keeping one's heart open.

We hugged our first-born, crying, and made our way back to our seats in time for Daniel to sing his havtorah section, a long passage in Hebrew that tells a sister story each Shabbat to the story told in the torah portion. Then everyone yelled out, "Mazel Tov" and wished him a sweet life by pelting him with candy. Daniel didn't duck, as most kids did. He just smiled, letting the chocolate kisses glance off his forehead and fall to the floor. An explosion of preschoolers shot out of the rows, rushing to cup handfuls of candy.

The dessert was magnificent: 20 fruit pies made by our friend Weedle, long-time winner of the Vinland Fair pie contest, and for good reason. Each cherry, blueberry, peach, and apple pie had lettering on the top spelling out "Daniel," or "Mazel Tov." They were accompanied by pizza pies (continuing our pie theme) in the big hall at the fairgrounds that my sisters and sisters-in-law had graciously decorated with blue crepe paper, candles, and fake floral centerpieces.

The decorations helped to soften the giant, bare room I had rented at a county office, filling out the forms while the office manager told me the long story of her breast reconstruction. Something had gone wrong, she said, pointing to her right breast, and now that breast leaned out the side instead of balancing nicely on her chest. She had to harness it forward every morning.

People swooped toward the pies and said things like, "These are the most beautiful pies I've ever seen" and "What a gorgeous sight." Everyone was a little hesitant to make the first cut, but once we encouraged them, the pies were ravaged almost as fast as the pizza. While the pie-eating was in full-force, I sat next to my father, who looked a little nervous and strangely quiet, and we tried to have one of our usual conversations, the one where we each ask each other how work was, and shrug a little.

He seemed more distant, and I didn't know if it was because he was shocked to find his oldest daughter bald in the middle of chemo, or just because he was always uncomfortable when visiting my world. I sat next to him, trying to make small talk about the business, his nice black suspenders, the flight from New Jersey. He stared at the crowd and, like a teenager, gave me a lot of one-word answers. Fine. Thanks. Okay.

Then the music started. We had hired a local group to first sing old rock-and-roll songs, and then Israeli and Hebrew songs. By the end of the night, we were circle- and line-dancing all over the concrete floor while Daniel, who loved music but hated the volume, stood outside talking to people.

After a few dances, I walked over to my dad and stepmother, who were surveying the dessert table, laden not just with pies but with a dozen or so other desserts added by friends. I knew my dad had diabetes, but he was planning to sample something anyway.

"If you're going to have anything," I said, pointing to a particularly potent chocolate cake, "have just a little taste of this. It's incredible."

He shook his head, and instead ferried a small square of sheet cake back to his table while I felt I had come up short again in finding some way to actually talk to him, to get beyond the smallest of small talk. At least, he didn't fall back into making a small joke about my cooking, child-rearing, or bald head that matched his own, only without the paste-on jewels. Time seemed so insistent and limited as I watched my father sit back down with his cake. Soon he would be gone, back to his home and work, and who knows when we would be face to face around a table full of desserts again.

Something about that moment matched the bittersweetness I felt when, earlier that day, we showed a video we had made for Daniel with photos from his whole life set to music. In one sequence of pictures, I had slipped in everyone we were close to who had died: my mother's father, who was a terrifically loving man named Abraham who had everyone call him Dave, holding a six-month-old Daniel; Ken's cousin, Janet, who had died at age 37 from cystic fibrosis, with a baby Daniel on her lap; Ken's grandmother, Elsa, and other relatives who had passed on.

The dead were there to help us celebrate, I thought, and to help us remember. I had no idea that my father, watching the video and eating a bagel with lox, would himself be dead six months later, living on only in photographs captured by one of the disposal cameras we'd scattered over the tables, photos that later would have the same weight as those of my grandfather, Ken's grandmother, and Janet. Or that Weedle, laughing as she drank her diet Pepsi and ate a slice of her own apple pie, would be killed in a car accident five years later. I had no idea when and how the earth would open up next.

Failing Genetics 101

Tina Johnson was a large woman with reddish hair and a kind handshake. She led Ken and me into a conference room at the hospital, which provided free genetic counseling to anyone who needed it. I wondered later if such counseling wasn't just a community service; it brought the hospital more business as those who tested positive would return for tests, probes, surgeries, and even nipple tattoos.

She sat us down at a giant conference table that circled the perimeter of the huge, freezing room. It was steamy outside, but Antarctica prevailed in genetic counseling land. She pulled a booklet from her beat-up briefcase and started giving us her spiel: what DNA did, how it was formed like a double helix, what BRCA 1 and BRCA 2 were, how they were related to other cancers, percentages of possible cancer occurrences, percentage of BRCA in the general public vs. among Ashkenazi Jews, options for surveillance or surgery. She had lists of questions to help her draw up a sloppy but somewhat accurate chart of cancer on both sides of my family.

Having the BRCA 1 genetic mutation would give a person a 87% chance of getting breast cancer in the first place, and a 67% chance of recurrence in addition to greatly increasing the odds of coming down with ovarian cancer. Furthermore, this mutation also added to the risk of pancreatic cancer.

"Now, if you do have the gene, and you choose to have the bilateral mastectomy, you can easily do reconstruction at the same time!"

"I don't think I want reconstruction," I said slowly, the chill in the room all over my cold arms. "I don't think it's what's right for me."

"Oh, there's nothing to be afraid of. The plastic surgeons here are wonderful, and you'll be in and out in no time."

"No, I don't really want to do that to my body."

"It won't hurt nearly as much as you think," she began, explaining details of how the procedure worked as if she had not heard what I said. "There's no reason to be afraid, and they can do a beautiful job of making you breasts. Any size you want, too."

I glanced at Ken, his face a study in control, and I could tell he was as amazed as I was that she didn't get what I was trying to say. But soon we were discussing the basic surgery, and she was explaining that doctors who performed an oophorectomy always removed the uterus as well. "Why take the uterus when it was an innocent bystander?" I wondered out loud. "Well, it's just sitting there" was her reply,

"Yeah, but why take it out when it's not any risk to me?"

I thought of how the highway project, if it succeeded, would take not only the land and right-of-way necessary for the freeway, but would also set up a domino-effect of erosion. Land that had nothing to do with the freeway, at first glance, would be changed from native tall grass prairie, with grass over my head that reddened and glowed in the winter, into something I couldn't yet imagine.

"It's not doing anything. And when they do it laproscopically, you'll be up and out in no time. I know a woman who, just a few days after her laparoscopic hysterectomy, was shopping in Wal-Mart like nothing ever happened."

I pictured a uterus-less woman aiming her cart past those smiley-face price signs. A woman who probably had a new pair of breasts too, "an upgrade," as an acquaintance later suggested to me. "Boy, I would do it if I could get one. And with a tummy tuck at the same time, all paid for by insurance. It sounds like heaven to me." At the time, we weren't at a Wal-Mart but at a Target, where she was viewing the new exercise clothes line. I sighed and said something about needing to get home.

"Look," said Tina back in genetic counseling. "Based on your family history, I'm sure you have the breast cancer gene. My question is whether you have it from one side of your family or both sides."

I felt myself falling off the planet again.

The more women I told about my possible array of surgery, the more surprising were the reactions I heard. Leaning against an old pickup truck at the state fair, two community activists, chain-smoking while joking with me about how to piss off the highway department even more, laughed off the thought of a double mastectomy.

"Me?" said Liz, who divided her time between herding her sheep and teaching ecology, "I would have them cut off and that's that. I'm sick to death of having these things. They're always in the way."

"I know exactly what you mean," said Lynn, a legal assistant who made a mean linguine. "Get them cut off, and be free! That's the way to go. I hate having boobs."

I was pretty depressed these days, feelings totally overwhelmed by the prediction that I would need to have all my female parts cut away. I wondered which part of my pain related to menopause, and which had settled in during the third round of chemo.

Of course, I could also chalk up my increasing depression to the chemicals swimming through my body, or maybe it had something to do with fear of death. It was so hard to tell.

I explained this to Dr. Stein over our pre-chemo tête-à-tête one summer day.

"Any of those reasons would be enough to be depressed. You want me to give you something?"

We had already tried some drug prescribed for hot flashes that was also supposed to wipe away any lingering sadness, but instead, it had made me feel like a character in *Night of the Living Dead*, and not one of the living ones.

"Nah, I don't want more drugs."

"That's smart, because whatever I gave you would take up to six weeks to really have any effect, and you'll be almost at your last chemo cycle by then."

"I'll be done one day?" I asked.

He shook his head and had me lie back for my breast exam.

"We have to stop meeting like this," he said, and we both smiled. Then he asked me about reconstructive surgery if I tested positive.

"No, I don't think so, but I'm not completely sure."

"It would be easier for you have the reconstruction. You like to camp and hike, and it would just be more convenient not to have to deal with prostheses."

Convenience. Like some kind of Kwik Shop product. "You know, I just don't think so."

By this time I was sitting up, off the table and back in my chair.

He leaned toward me. "Just promise me you'll at least speak to the plastic surgeon and learn more about your options."

I half-nodded. I probably wouldn't, but then again, should I? Having nice round breasts and a flatter stomach was tempting.

"I don't know what to do," I told Ursula on the phone. I was opening drawers and cabinets, looking for the colander. Our new sitter, who was also charged with helping out around the kitchen, had a talent for putting all the plates, pots, and bowls in different places each time. Other people who dropped in and helped also made their own rules about what went where.

I tried to explain more to her, but I was caught up in sadness again by the errant shoes in the living room, the blanket draped on the dining room floor, the papers all over the counter, the spilled juice hardening into a kind of sticky linoleum on the table. I still couldn't find the colander, let alone figure out what to do about cleaning up and straightening out my body.

"It's okay. You'll find your own answers," she answered.

Clean or Die

I got home from my session with Ursula, where a realization—more like a flashing headline—came to me while I was lying on the treatment table: that my house was my body, the garden and yard, too. This flash filled me with a purpose, and, given the state of my home, with a kind of nightmare. If the house was the body, and the body, the house, what did it mean for me to live in a place swaddled in disorder and dirty dishes, old newspapers, and a corner in the basement where the dog repeatedly peed? Determined, I walked into a house gone chaotic.

Ken, working full-time and commuting, and the kids—hot, tired, and often distracted by the new television and VCR—hadn't done more than make spaghetti and eat it in the playroom with the TV blasting for several days. I looked at the kitchen, the living room, the dining room—all demonstrating far too clearly to me how, if the house was body, I was in serious trouble. I realized part of this was my fault for putting what energy I had into organizing the congress or writing evaluations of my students (what we do at Goddard instead of giving grades), but I wasn't in the mood to turn any more blame inward at the moment.

"We've got to clean right now," I yelled at my family, snapping off the television set where they'd been watching cartoons. I stepped on spaghetti, smashed into the carpet, to illustrate my point. "Our house is out of control, and we need to stop living like this. I just can't take it anymore!"

"Hey, we're watching that," Natalie yelled back.

"Yeah," said Ken, "We'll clean after dinner."

"No, you won't. Everyone, get up and clean right now! Daniel, where are you going? Get back upstairs," I told my son, who was edging downstairs toward the computer. "Everyone get up right now and start cleaning. Natalie, you do the bathrooms. Ken, you sweep and vacuum. Daniel, get started on the dishes. Forest, get up from behind the couch," I said to my cowering younger son, "and start cleaning your room, right now!!!"

My family just stared back at me blankly, glancing at each other with that look of deep conspiracy.

"I mean it! Get up now and clean this house! You have to do this now!"

No one budged, and in fact, they started yelling back, telling me to chill out, get a grip, leave them alone, I was overreacting.

I wouldn't let go and ended up fleeing to the bathroom, where I discovered that the boys had missed the toilet again, and clothes and newspapers lay on the floor. The words that flew out of my mouth were mostly four-lettered and loud. I considered cleaning the whole house myself, just doing it all, and even started picking up plates and cups to dump them in the sink, but partway through, exhaustion flared up in me, and it was all I could do to get myself to the bedroom and crawl across the bed, furious and determined not to cry, not to break.

I wasn't thinking about the chemo, how it was currently erasing my periods and tornadoing my hormones, or about the genetic testing, my family, and this land. All I could see were thousands of small cleaning tasks that needed my full attention now.

"Trying to make changes without compassion kills everything," Ken told me a few hours later as he sat beside me on the floor of our bedroom—also a mess—with his hand on my back. By this time, I was crying and so depressed over how we lived that I didn't believe I would ever recover, or get to sleep. "Whatever we do, we have to do it compassionately because we're going to keep failing in big and little ways all the time."

He sat down next me, and I put my head on his lap. Usually, he would stroke my hair at such a time, but since I was hairless, he gently put his hand on my forehead and exhaled.

No Picnic

Broccoli spanakopita, hummus, french fries, artichoke salad, and cheesecake with cherries on top. That was what we ate as we sat at the picnic table— faculty from my program, and the faculty from another program sharing our summer residency at the college. We were in Vermont in August, and the world was shining with roses and lilies and sunflowers all in bloom at once. As for the food, since our meals were prepared by chefs from a local culinary institute, such eclectic mixtures were common.

A new faculty member from the other program, an artist named Catherine, sat across from me, explaining how during her chemo a year ago for breast cancer she was outrageously depressed all the time. John said that his boyfriend, a performance artist like himself, had a horrible time with Hodgkin's lymphoma. They had freaked out when the boyfriend's body hair fell out, but then they got into body painting. Another faculty member told of her partner being so sick from chemo that, at one point, all her body functions started shutting down. After three rounds (she was supposed to have four), she stopped going to chemo and just went on to radiation, and all this following a bilateral mastectomy that showed she had cancer in both breasts.

I told everyone all my symptoms, and they nodded sympathetically. Meanwhile, we ate our cheesecake slowly, talking about art, cancer, students, weather.

Later that week, after the students arrived, I found myself functioning on auto-pilot, not all there but trying as hard as I could to act like I still had some intelligence, could still listen well, could say something of value. Repeatedly, though, I found myself nodding when people talked to me, trying to act as if I were present when I really didn't know where I was, and later couldn't remember what the conversation was about.

My students, however, were particularly caring. In my small, corner office with windows overlooking the dark green foliage and wide open lawn between the manor house and the road, they told me that they were ready to study what writing could show them about living with serious illness, or how they wanted to tell stories to help people connect more with the earth. Sitting there with students, one at a time as we discussed what they wished to study this coming semester, which books could be of use, how they might write a memoir or create a portfolio of photography, I slowly found ways to come back to the earth where I was, and to hear them more fully.

Yet somehow the residency schedule, which kept faculty and students working like dogs from sun-up to sundown, didn't fit me anymore, like a shirt that had shrunk in the wash. So I ended up sneaking off to my dorm room and taking a lot of naps, occasionally asking other faculty to teach my workshop or speak to a student for me. Luckily, everyone encouraged me to nap frequently, which was particularly thrilling when faced with the choice between a drawn-out faculty meeting or a roll in dreamland.

One afternoon, waking from my nap, I looked into the mirror to see my bald head, my big eyes, the circles beneath them. I looked into my eyes for a while, and that was a massive mistake, but I didn't know it at the time. My eyes seemed darker, browner, more like my father's eyes. The more I looked, the more frightened I became. What if I were dying right now? What if the chemo wasn't working? What if this was just the beginning of years of agony, pain, loss and atrophy?

The fear of death poured out of me with such force that it seemed to have no end. I felt shaky and terrified, and yet I had a hard time turning away from the mirror. The mirror held a reflection that shook me out of my normal sense of reality, the sense of well-being I had preserved despite all the dangers around and within my body.

I found Francis, one of my colleagues, a consciousness studies expert from Montreal who, when he wasn't teaching, made a mean curry. "I'm afraid I could die," I told him as we sat in the run-down living room of the faculty dorm. He nodded, affirming it was possible, and then signaled me to come walk with him to the cafeteria for dinner.

"What if I do?" I asked him as we walked arm-in-arm through the first falling leaves from the otherwise green maples.

"You'll find out what happens then," he answered, and I felt more scared.

Whimsy as usual intervened as soon as we were seated at a table with our trays of dinner. A woman, highly-made-up and be-wigged, walked over to me in the college cafeteria and started mooning over my tattoos.

"Oh, you're so brave to do that. I have alopecia and I wish I could do that. I just hate this wig."

She went on to tell me that she had had her eyebrows tattooed on, and did I know that some women who go through chemo never get their hair back?

The next night I heard applause coming from a corner of the cafeteria and there she was, at a circular table full of happy, clapping people. She had removed her wig and she looked great, like an Amazon version of Sigourney Weaver in her Alien role. "It's no picnic," I heard her tell them when I was on my way for tofu cheesecake with a side of fries and hot fudge.

Breast Envy

The breasts are buffers, padding between bone and air, heart and sky, earth and head. My breasts were born and grew up when I was between 15 and 16, in central New Jersey. Size 32 AAA, eventually 36A, then 38C during pregnancy to 40ish C now. Triangle danglers. Soft kittens.

My breasts always seemed too small or funny-shaped in my twenties, not like the round and full breasts in magazines. I used to joke that I had enough room to stick a third breast in the middle of the two I had. But after

Daniel was born, all that changed. When my milk dropped in the hospital room where Ken and I were crying because we were exhausted and had a new baby in intensive care, we marveled at how huge the breasts suddenly became.

"Just like Dolly Parton," he said.

"I should have a little cart to carry them around on," I answered. Truth be told, it was tough to walk around with those giant rocks made of milk, round and aching, from hospital room to intensive care where I could hold the baby but could not yet nurse him, and then to a small room where a giant mother-milking machine was attached to me that filled up little glass bottles in less than 10 minutes.

From then on, it seemed my breasts grew closer together, literally, and I suddenly had curves, depth, weight. I bought bigger bras, and casually named them Mr. Breast and Mrs. Breast even though previously I had found it absolutely the depth of ludicrousness to name any body part. Still, the Mr. and Mrs. worked well to remind myself which side the baby last nursed on and which side was ready to head back into the game.

After weaning Daniel, then Natalie, and finally Forest, my breasts didn't really shrink again but stayed in the C-cup range, nicely balancing out the accumulating fat below my waistline. I grew to like them, very much actually, and I especially appreciated how going through childbirth and nursing had sensitized them tremendously. They were an important part of my sex life, and a vital part of what made me feel sensual, certainly in the top five or so of fun body parts. I was aware of them often and felt like we were thoroughly bonded and living quite happily, sometimes even ecstatically, together.

Now I sat in Dr. Stein's treatment room while the nurse cleaned my port and Dr. Stein gently handed me the single piece of paper with my test results. Although my mother had called me last night and said she had tested negative, my report clearly showed that I was positive. I had the BRCA genetic mutation, BRCA 1 to be exact.

"It's what you thought," he said.

"You know, my mom tested negative, but she had breast cancer, and so did my aunt."

"It could be on your dad's side, or her test could have been false." He touched the top of my hand, looking at me as if this was truly horrible news. Judy, sitting beside me in a red silk blouse, held her breath. Ken reached out for my shoulder. Strangely, I didn't feel sad or angry, didn't feel much more than, "Oh, this is what I thought would happen." Acceptance or denial? Sometimes there's no way to tell.

All through that chemo treatment that followed that day, Dr. Stein checked in on me, surprised I was so nonchalant. For weeks afterwards, I was on the lookout for grief to suddenly sideswipe me, but it never happened… at least not for many, many months. Maybe the most intense part of the mourning was behind me, I thought, or maybe it would unfurl years later.

I had already read all the descriptions of reconstruction—how skin could be moved from the stomach or the back (both places where I had ample amounts to contribute) to mold into little mounds. How implants could be put in and injected slowly, over time, with saline fluid, or slipped already fully-fueled beneath the skin.

I could not envision any of this without thinking of the proposed freeway, suburban sprawl, urban decay, or how, when we moved from Brooklyn to New Jersey when I was eight, the housing developer had created a small, fake hill in the backyard of each home. Some of our neighbors decorated their hills with shrines to the Virgin Mary, others with play houses for their kids, or just a clump of low-lying cedar that never looked at home atop the mini hill.

Women at the Jewish Community Center services joked about my getting perky new boobs. Women in magazine articles about breast cancer always praised their rebuilds. Anyone I, or my friends and family, knew who had had a mastectomy had chosen a rebuild, including the volunteers from the cancer support groups who called me after surgery to offer support. When I went to various chat rooms to talk with others going through what I was going through, I found, again and again, that it was rare as snow in July for a woman to refuse reconstruction. In fact, on the one web site I found a woman who hadn't done the rebuild, but then she decided to go back in and have it done a year or two later.

Yet I also heard many stories of reconstructions gone bad. A woman in a department store where I was trying on sundresses one day, said her implants hardened and were excruciatingly painful so she had to get them removed, and now she was trying to figure out what new kind of implant to put in. Someone told me her best friend couldn't sit up for a month after the tram surgery (moving skin from the stomach to the breast). A bioregionalist from Maine wrote me about her mom's botched surgery that led to five more surgeries, none of which worked.

Most disturbing of all was how everyone said their new breasts had no real feeling in them, no sensual life like they had before.

Ken and I sat down at Zen Zero, a local restaurant, to eat our stir-fry. The mustard yellow walls and fast-moving waiters seemed to swirl around us. He looked concerned.

"You can do whatever you want, and you know that I'll support you no matter what you choose."

I nodded, forked up some chicken and rice.

"But I would rather you didn't do the reconstruction. Your body has been through enough, and you don't need to do this for me."

Already, he had told me repeatedly, in response to the question that I had asked well over 100 times about whether he needed or wanted me to have breasts, that it really didn't matter to him.

"I don't need you to do this for me," he answered almost daily when I asked.

I knew what he was saying was true—that my body, having faced surgery already, and now in the last throes of chemo with more surgery ahead—didn't need extra cutting and moving, molding and sculpting simply to make little mounds to fill my bra or look somewhat natural from a distance. I thought about the lumpectomy, the sentinel node biopsy, the lymph node dissection, the port installation, the chemo, the weekly needles to draw blood, and everything else.

I thought, too, about how for me at least, there was something unecological about moving parts of the body around like they were pieces of real estate. Yet I could also understand the desire to do reconstruction, to set up nicely shaped, always-perky (like even when you're in your eighties) breasts that I wouldn't have to mess with. The appeal of losing some of the extra fat below my waist was, well, enormously appealing.

But already I knew and had known all along, what my body would say if it could speak up for itself, and it would say, "no rebuild." After so much of my life spent not listening to my body, taking refuge in the tree house of my mind—which was outfitted with VCR, books, magazines, and lots of food—part of my lesson, or maybe all of it concerned listening to my body, and not letting the mini-dictator in the front lobe do all the driving.

There was something else just as significant to me: the importance of looking at this loss head-on, of seeing myself breastless every day, every night, and making peace with it. I wanted to learn to love my body in a whole new way, more than I had ever been able to love it before. Listening to what my body wanted, what my body didn't want, was the first lesson in making that love more of a verb than an abstraction.

"No, I'm not going to do a rebuild," I told him as we walked out of the restaurant. We held hands and slowly walked around in an old neighborhood. The air cooling off just enough to make it bearable, and the flowers spilling out of broken pots.

My Alligator Ate My Cell Phone

We entered the cell phone store in great fear and trepidation, having heard all the stories about people losing cell phones, and then having to pay $200 or more to make up for the loss. I felt nauseous that morning anyway, and it didn't help that it was nearly 100 degrees. I was kicking myself for failing to buy that cell phone insurance. Ken was quiet too, especially since it was his cell phone that was lost, probably in a movie theater, but it was hard to say for sure. My theory was that it was traveling on the floor of the car with us, having fallen out of his pocket, and at some point, it flung itself out the door hoping to be reincarnated as a laptop.

But for us that day, the real question concerned economic suicide. Did we replace this phone—this lifeline between Ken and me during our chemo-ized life these days—when the medical bills were ambling in, and my income was down to a slow trickle? We had spent more than the usual amount on activities and childcare for the kids that summer, trying to cover my stretches of exhaustion. Cancer was expensive, I thought to myself as I perused the gleaming red and black cell phones, each one as shiny as a new car, that coated the walls of the cell phone store.

As usual there was a wait, and I filled it by worrying about the money hole cancer was digging in our lives. I counted on my fingers and in my head, calculating something like $8,000 in lost income and extra medical bills. What I didn't know then was that by the time I finished treatment, it would easily total twice that much, and would propel me toward dimly-lit discount stores probably populated by visitors from other planets, where we would fill our cart with whatever was on sale.

I turned to check on how long it would be before the cell phone associates, a young man in spiffy slacks and a non-threatening tie, or a young woman in navy with her lovely blond hair in a tight French knot, might wait on us. That's when I saw the alligator.

A woman about my age, decked out in worn T-shirt and shorts, and a pack of cigarettes sticking out her T-shirt pocket, walked through the door carrying an alligator. This was too good to be true. I rushed over to her and her husband immediately.

"Is that really an alligator?" I stupidly asked.

"Sure is," she said, with the hoarseness that gave away that she was a heavy smoker. Of course, I might be a heavy smoker, too, if I lived with an alligator.

"The little fella chewed up the cell phone," her husband piped up, "and I figured they're never gonna believe this unless we bring him in." The man held up a mangled dark blue cell phone.

Of course, I had to ask and they had to explain that they were feeding Theodore, the alligator, when the cell phone fell out of the guy's shirt pocket and into the tank.

"None of our friends can believe it," the woman said. "And I knew this place," she said, gesturing toward the neatly-clad, not very attentive cell phone workers, "would never in a million years believe me if I didn't bring this guy in."

Ken and I were petting the alligator by this time, feeling its particular soft shell exterior and looking curiously at Theodore's crocked jaw with all those sharp teeth. The woman held Theodore, the three or so feet of him pressed up against her body like a large, complacent toddler.

"He's just a sweetheart. Now aren't you, hon?" she crooned.

"Oh, he's just a big baby. We love him to death."

We had to ask what he ate (rodents), where he slept (in his tank), and what he did for fun (occasionally, they let him wander around the house, and he especially liked stretching out on the window seat). Our encounter with the alligator was abruptly interrupted when the supervisor, a slightly older woman who had obviously dealt with her share of irate cell phone customers in the past and had the weary eyes to prove it, came over.

"You're going to have to get that…that thing, out of the store immediately," she said. I looked back to see the young cell phone attendants backed up against the wall of phones, looking very concerned. "It's a public danger."

"Oh, he's just a big old pussycat," the man said, "and besides, we wanted to prove to you what happened to the cell phone."

"You've proved it," she said quickly. "Now please, get it out of the store this minute before I have to call the police."

The couple shrugged, and I removed my hand from the happy alligator's head. The woman carried Theodore out to the pickup truck where he would cuddle in her lap while she waited.

"Now," said the woman looking at us, "You're next. How can we help you?"

We had nothing quite so dramatic to report—only a cell phone suicide and not an attack by a wild animal, but report it we did. To our surprise, it only cost $19.95 to replace the kamikaze cell phone, with no penalties or extensions of our contract.

We exchanged a high five on the way to the car, and waved goodbye to the alligator in the car parked beside us. We might be heading toward financial ruin, but not without some alligators along for the ride.

News Flash

A month before the congress, we met at our house as we had been doing over the last year and a half, gathering in the living room with an easel, giant pad and markers, and piles of food just around the corner in the kitchen, waiting for us and nudging us toward completion. Rita had arrived a few days before, and would simply stay until the congress, living at Mark's house where she set up her food-ordering-meal-planning world headquarters, complete with charts, maps, lists and already, some 40-pound sacks of rice and oatmeal at her feet. Jerry and I had been calling each other almost hourly to report late-breaking registrations, or brainstorm on how to pick up someone who was hopping a freight train to land near the camp somewhere in the neighborhood of 2 a.m.

We listened to Ken talk about talking circles, small groups every congress-goer would participate in each morning, a kind of way to start the day by listening to one another and being listened to before the onslaught of workshops, large group and committee meetings. Although the air-conditioner, a window unit we snagged at a yard sale, was on full blast behind me, and I had a fan aimed toward me, I still felt like the wicked witch after Dorothy threw water on her.

"So we need to come up with about 20 plants and animals of this region because we're going to name each talking circle after a native specie," Ken explained. I scooped an ice cube out of the water and gently held it on top of my head, and looked around the room.

"Bobcat," Joy said.

"Coyote," Rita added. She was standing up fast, pulling her shirt off, and sitting back down in her sleeveless shirt.

"Isn't the chigger a native specie?" Joy asked, making some of us laugh. I noticed Joy didn't seem hot, and when I looked around the circle—Curtis, Jerry, Mark, Danny—I realized a few of them had put on sweaters or light jackets. Rita, on the other hand, was fanning herself furiously with her stack of menu plans.

"Big bluestem," said Curtis, "And you know, we should have Butterfly Milkweed too. That's one of my favorites."

"And insects, let's not shortchange them because they really run the world," Danny added.

"What about spiders?" Ken asked.

My skin suddenly was clammy. I hated spiders although I could pet a snake any day, but I hadn't seen a snake in a long time. Weren't snakes a female fertility symbol according to Ursula? I tried to remember, and then it occurred to me. I hadn't had a period since before this chemo round. In the heat and congress-organizing, the Highway 59 fight and driving children to swimming lessons, the pills before bed and pills with breakfast, I had somehow slipped through the door of menopause, and without noticing. I had left my old, fertile self behind.

"What about deer? Are they too common?" Mark asked.

"Buffalo!" said Jerry.

"Tree frog," said Rita.

My skin seemed to heat up all over again although I was just in shorts and a tank top and it was actually cool outside today, overcast and in the 60s.

"Okay, let's keep brainstorming," Ken said. "Caryn, you got anything?"

I looked across at Rita, who was smiling and lifting up her over-shirt to slip back over her head.

"Hot flash," I said, realizing I was now in the Hot Flash talking circle, trying to listen to what new temperate climates my body was chattering about incessantly.

"You Look Great!"

That was what people said, often and always, when they saw me in public. I could be buying some bagels or walking through the grocery store; I could be drinking tea in a coffee shop or emerging from a showing of *My Big Fat Greek Wedding*, which I saw four times during chemo, my need to laugh so great that I would do anything repeatedly that helped. Over and over I heard, "You look great!"

I didn't know what people with cancer were supposed to look like, but I got the impression that simply because I could leave the house, wearing God-knows-what, I looked great. I might feel like shit, but I looked great, and I usually loved it whenever people told me this, which was good because it happened every day, many times.

One day, in particular, I had heard repeatedly that I looked great. Unfortunately, my interior wasn't matching my exterior, and I was queasy with little digestive jolts that sent me to bathrooms in a hurry. Considering it was also the day the Highway 59 group released its shadow Environmental Impact Statement to the press, I worried how I would get through the press conference taking place in the main rotunda of the courthouse, a floor down from the rest rooms.

Luckily, my body calmed down, and so I stood with the others, wearing a red cap over my bald head because I thought it might look more professional than my shark tattoos, and started reading the statement for the group. The newspaper reporters and photographer listened, shifting around to get new shots or arrange interviews with various members of the group. There were 10 of us clustered together that day. We held our stacks of paper high, with the narratives and detailed studies we had done, piece by piece, late at night over several weeks, making a whole out of everything.

"So is your group completely opposed to any highway renovation?" a reporter asked.

"No, that's never been our stance. We simply want Highway 59 widened on Highway 59."

The reporter pretended not to notice I was bald, but within minutes a photographer, a jaunty young man with a deep cleft in his chin, asked us to stand closer for a picture. "Ma'am, would you like to take off your hat?"

Miriam took my arm and shook her head, and Bruce started to laugh a little.

"Um, I'm bald. I'm going through chemo for breast cancer."

The photographer looked up from his camera. "Oh, sorry. My mom had that. I'm really sorry."

"You look great," the reporter said, trying to be helpful.

A few evenings later, I sat on Forest's bed, counting backwards from 100, an old sleeping story trick a friend taught me. I would count in tens, saying there were 10 kangaroos named 100, 99, 98, and so on, naming a new animal for each decade of numbers. Usually he was sleeping before I reached the teens.

"Mom, I'm really awake tonight so you should start with a higher number," he said, a fleece blanket under him and one above him too.

"What should I start with?"

"One billion and three. That would be a good number."

I started with 100, and he was again sleeping by 14.

As I slipped out of his room, I crashed into Daniel, heading to bed himself in the room the boys shared.

"Mom, you don't look so great," he said.

I didn't feel so great either, and it wasn't just the chemo and steroids, but a growing uneasiness about whether this was ever going to end. I felt as if a giant machine from Mars had landed in our field, attached a tentacle to my torso when I was sleeping, and sucked out all my energy.

A few hours later, lying beside Ken, I said, "I can't stand it anymore, I feel so weak that I just can't stand it."

"I know," he said, "but you're getting through this." He lay next to me. Later, he would tell me he had been holding in his own flood of fear and sadness, in the same way as he carefully withheld the news that a woman he worked with had just died of breast cancer. I still don't know how he did it.

At the time, though, I just said, "No, I'm not, and it's lasting forever."

We were in the middle of chemo cycle number four, and there were at least two more months of treatment. The heat was above 100 degrees, and I didn't have the strength to do much. Even loading the dishwasher seemed like climbing a 14,000-foot mountain in Chinese slippers...during a thunder storm. Sitting up and watching a movie felt like, well, loading a dishwasher.

"I'm so sad, and I don't know why."

He wrapped his arms and legs around me as I sobbed into my already-wet pillow.

A few weeks later, home from a goodbye picnic for dear friends who were moving away, I was sitting on the bed, talking with Ken, when this wave of fear suddenly swept over me. I started shaking, and my jaw was trembling so hard it hurt. The terror encompassed all of me, and I was afraid it was so fierce that I was actually starting to go out of my mind, and not funny-bonkers crazy, but institutional-insane crazy.

I managed to get enough words out to ask Ken to sit behind me and hold me tight. In a few minutes, the terror passed as quickly as it had come.

A week later, I was visiting some friends, sitting in a chair in their living room, when the terror came again, not quite as strongly, but enough that I could only pretend I was listening to the conversation while inside I felt myself trembling into an oblivion made of all my fears: the fear of death, the fear of living and dying at once too young, and the fear of something I couldn't actually name. Fear that possessed the vigor of a tornado swooping down, and just as mysteriously, lifting back up and disappearing.

"You look great," one of my friends said as my terror storm ended. I nodded and smiled, unable to explain that inside I felt like I was crossing a vast desert. It was hot, there was no water around, there was little or no shade, some wind, but often hot and searing. I could barely see before me the edge of what might be a forest in the distance, a two months' walk from here. I could no longer see the green lushness where I had started this journey, almost 100 days ago. I was tired of having so many strange dreams, a cornucopia of bizarre images bombarding me each night. I was tired of having toxic chemicals move through my body. I was tired of not knowing my body these days, yet having to listen to my body, lie down when it said to lie down, get quiet when it said to get quiet, eat when it said to eat, like I'd never listened before.

The Rice Paddies of Cancer

Driving home down the long road that led to our driveway, the rich evening quiet and lovely in its blueness around me, I had a strange feeling that something awful was going to happen. First the car accident, and now cancer. It seemed to me that a third bad thing was coming my way, because wasn't it true that bad things came in threes? I teased myself for thinking such stupid thoughts. We've been through enough, and I didn't have to imagine anything else.

I walked into the house, excited from having given a poetry reading as part of the Healing and Hope event for the first anniversary of the September 11th tragedy, and feeling feverish from the neupogen.

"Call your sister," Ken told me. "She really wants to talk to you."

"But it's like 11:00 back there," I said, remembering that she lived in Orlando.

"She said to call her anyway."

She answered the phone immediately just as I was putting down a pile of papers and settling in.

"You're not going to believe this, but Dad has pancreatic cancer."

"What do you mean he has pancreatic cancer? How can this be true?"

Both Lauren and I knew well that pancreatic cancer, a fairly rare form of cancer and certainly one of the most deadly, had killed our Uncle Howard, my dad's brother, about five years ago. What was the chance of it showing up twice in a family?

"He's in the hospital now. They're running tests. He was having some stomach problems, and they thought he had food poisoning or something."

"Oh my god."

"But it's pancreatic cancer, and he's lost like 25 pounds already."

I had just seen him a few months earlier at the Bar Mitzvah, seemingly fine, seemingly the same. How could he have been dying all along?

That night, I crawled into bed astonished. My father, relatively young for the parent of a 42-year-old, was dying. The man with whom I had struggled for years was not going to live very long. The man I always thought would be around for decades, the relationship I figured we had decades to deal with.

The next day, Ken and I researched pancreatic cancer, me at the home computer where the bad news arrived at the slow, take-a-long-breath speed of dial-up, and him at his job, where the details of impending loss jolted onto the screen. About 29,000 people got it each year, and of those 29,000, less than 100 were still alive by the year's end. I learned about the shape of the pancreas, what it did, what a whipple operation was, and found a list-serv for people with pancreatic cancer and their families. Some patients were able to discuss their recovery from the difficult whipple operation, but most of those had had the surgery within the last year or two, and many now had new complications. "It's in my liver," seemed to be a tragic refrain.

"It's the only kind of cancer without a survivor organization," Victoria told me. I was pacing on my deck in the twilight, talking with her on the phone, trying to make sense of this spectacularly stark thing happening.

"Okay, so I'm horrified, and I can't believe this is happening," I told her. "But on the other hand, I keep thinking, 'no new injuries.' Is that sick or what?"

"Hey, it makes sense given what you've been through with your dad. Just remember that death doesn't end anything. Your relationship with him will go on, just like mine did with my dad," she said. I remembered her father, a kind man who conspired with me to pour an anisette-flavored liquor into hot cocoa one Christmas season 20 years ago, who fed me buttery cookies and laughed about the richness of this moment with me. I also remembered how her mother had lived through breast cancer to become an astonishing landscape painter of the prairie, and now the Southwest.

A few days later, I called my dad for the update, ready to just hang out with whatever pain or fear was occupying him. But he was unexpectedly upbeat.

"It's going to be okay. They have this new operation, this special whipple, and it should clean out all the cancer," he told me. His rendition sounded like an infomercial pitching a cleaning gizmo that scoured drains and sliced carrots.

"Are you going to have to do chemo?" I asked, remembering how when I started treatment, my father didn't know the difference between chemo and radiation.

"I don't know, but the thing is, I can beat this. I just have to have the surgery."

The doctor also told him the cancer had spread to his gallbladder, and because of his sleep apnea, heart condition, and diabetes, they were holding up surgery—a new, so-called revolutionary procedure—until his health improved. They might even operate on the sleep apnea first.

We talked then about BRCA, and he said he would get tested next week. He insisted he had BRCA because his brother died of this cancer and now he had it, too. "The bottom line is, I ain't gonna die."

I hung up the phone telling myself I was going to lose my father within the next year, maybe the next six months. My breasts and my father—impending losses. I thought I had some understanding of losing my breasts but I had no idea of the magnitude of losing a parent.

That night, I dreamt I was walking down paths among rice paddies in a very lush, rolling green landscape. I turned around, and I saw my father behind me. He dove down into the water, which suddenly turned very deep, and went under. I remember thinking how strange it was that he didn't change his clothes, but when I woke, I realized he didn't have time to change—either his clothes or his life. The rice paddy seemed like cancer to me, or some kind of trial, one that I was just ankle-deep in now, but into which my father had to dive completely without much chance of emerging.

Bird Song

I lay on the table in Ursula's treatment room, now most of the way through chemo round number five, with the last round just around the corner, just before my trip to the Flint Hills for the long-awaited Continental Bioregional Congress. I would be done by that time, and I could stop shaving my head which grew only sparse, black fuzz toward the end of each chemo cycle. All summer I had been dragging the razor, carefully, over my head once a week, getting rid of my five-o'clock shadow before applying a new round of temporary tattoos.

Today, I was wearing a tattoo collection from the hit parade, one everyone liked: birds. I had a cardinal, blue jay, hawk, eagle, dove, junco and a few others I couldn't identify pasted carefully in a garland around my nice round head. I closed my eyes, counting the days until my final chemo session, until the Congress, until I would be growing hair and giving up shaving, until I would be normal again.

Ursula started with my feet as usual, holding my toes, breathing. I relaxed slightly, but kept counting. Eleven days until final big infusion. Eighteen days until the final little infusion. Twenty-one days until the congress. She walked to the other end of the table and placed her hands on my forehead. I breathed with her. My head hurt, and so did my stomach. I was tired, exhausted actually, and there was still so much to do after chemo—more surgery and recovery, and what else?

I didn't know what else, because I started seeing birds. Maybe I imagined them, maybe not. A red-winged blackbird over my forehead. Two tired and scared doves for my breasts. Herons and bluebirds and crows. An owl in my throat, asleep. The bluebirds in my clavicle area, near the chemo port. And the red-winged blackbird by my forehead. All the birds were there to help me. I heard bird song from outside, and felt the presence of birds all over my body, quiet creatures perched on the branches of my being.

Then I thought of my mother, and how hard it must be for her to know I had this cancer. I imagined reassuring her, but to my surprise, I felt a sudden flood of joy and acceptance of anything, even death. Death, which I'd always been scared to even think about suddenly seemed utterly exciting, mysterious, beautiful even. It would be an adventure of a proportion beyond our trip to Africa, where Ken and I had traveled in the mid-1980s. I had never felt anything like this before, and I had no words to contain the thrill of it.

But death wasn't what I wanted. In my mind, I said, over and over, "I choose life." And just to make it utterly clear, "I choose a long, long life."

Afterwards, I sat up and moved to the white chair opposite Ursula to talk about what happened. "I saw birds," I told her, "all over me."

She smiled. It turned out that she had been remembering a song, hearing the tune in her mind when she worked on me, that she had learned in Germany about the little bird sitting at my foot, carrying greetings from its mother. She sang me the German version softly, her blue eyes shining, and then told me the translation. A lost bird. A bird trying to return to her mother.

That night, I overheard Daniel and Forest talking in their bedroom across the hall from ours.

"God sees everything," said Daniel.

"Are you sure?" asked Forest.

"He saw you scratch me. He saw you bring me an ice cream bar. He saw Mom in surgery. He saw all of us being born."

There was a pause, then Forest spoke again. "Did God see God being born?"

Chemo Is Cumulative

The infusion was a few days ago, and now, between the steroid dexamethasone to speed me up, the lorizipan to slow me down, and some other mind-numbing drugs—a designer-mix, the improved-life-through-chemistry alternative to holding a bucket in my hands and throwing up for a few days—I felt like I was going to jump out of my skin. Judy and I sat in the coffee shop, nursing iced mochas. I put my hand on the window, already hot from the near-100 degree afternoon of this late August day.

All week, the Highway 59 group had been submerged in meetings, emails, and phone calls to discuss the news that the highway department had decided not to widen the highway on its present route, but to build a freeway 400 feet to the east. While 400 feet was better than a mile, this alternative meant that woodlands, prairies, Native American sites, and even Santa Fe Trail ruts wouldn't be disturbed. But one freeway built so close to another highway would still create a development corridor. We had won, sort of, a half victory, and we couldn't decide what to do. Ken and I would lie in bed at night, puzzling over whether we should go on fighting or end our four-year-old highway battle.

The indecision of the group reinforced the general indecision where I was living lately. I had just spent the morning lying in bed, with no desire to get up, no desire to go to sleep. I kept trying to decide what to do. All my readings over the years of Buddhist theology applauded the point of no desire, but now that I was there, it was nothing like I expected: it was merely a place of intense boredom and restlessness at war with each other. Over the last few days, I found myself watching clocks, praying for time to pass. Coupled with this were bouts of intense stomach cramping and occasional spells of either constipation or diarrhea.

I felt like I lived in a psychic blender.

"If there were a balloon above your head like in a cartoon, it would have two people in it, fighting," Judy said.

I held my decaf skinny mocha deluxe on the rocks, wondering why in the hell I ordered this. It was all wrong.

"Huh?"

"A balloon above your head."

"Oh, like in a cartoon."

She rolled her eyes.

I looked out the window, down at the magazine on the table, tried to take a sip of the drink that was all wrong, looked out the window again, and back at Judy. I felt like a very stupid tiny bird that had left its nest too young.

"What is going on with you? You're all over the place," she said.

"I don't know. I feel like I'm going out of my mind."

"One more round of chemo, and you're done, kiddo. Remember, it's cumulative."

I had called my mother earlier, trying to make coherent sentences, but she kept telling me that maybe I should rest and call back later. I had tried to answer emails for the bioregional congress, just a few weeks away, but I made so many typos that I gave up trying.

At nightfall, I pulled a kitchen chair out to the deck, where I sat, staring at the cottonwood tree, envying its ability to sway and yet stay rooted. I wished for my mind, which was obviously gone on a rock 'n roll road trip without me, to come back, unpack, and tell me where it had been.

The cicadas started up again like a train slowly roaring into the station, low and then loud until I felt like the sound came from inside my head as well as outside. Then the roaring would diminish for just a few seconds before returning. Waves of sound poured from the woods, but I knew that soon, when the sun slipped just a little lower behind the ridge of trees in the west, when the chill returned to the night air, the cicadas would leave.

Ken pulled out a chair and sat next to me, neither of us talking. He had already told me that this year was a banner cicada year, with the 13- and 17-year cicada cycles coinciding. It made for a wall of sound so fierce that it would keep me awake in the afternoons. "What do they look like?" I asked Ken, realizing, that to me, the cicadas were more like some invisible, mystical woodland critter.

He walked down the stairs and went to the nearest tree, returning with the shell of one, a black husk with sheer, lacy wings. The roar swept over us again, a cumulative echo we lived in, unable, for the moment, to say anything that the other would be able to hear.

Goner

The night before we were to fly to New Jersey for my sister Jennifer's wedding, Aunt Rhoda called. I was in the basement, powering down the computer after three hours of answering emails from more congress attendees, and sending packets to all 107 who had so far registered. Now all I needed to do was pack our toiletries for the trip. "Yeah, Aunt Rhoda. How you doing?" I asked.

"Don't go. Jen is in the hospital and the wedding is off," my aunt told me.

"She's what? How can this be?"

"She had an attack of pancreatitis. They had to cancel the wedding, but Eric is there with her."

I sank into my chair, talked over every detail she knew, got instructions to call my sister Lauren, who was visiting with my dad in Pennsylvania, and tried to call my mother. She must have been at the hospital because her cell phone didn't work.

I did reach my dad's house, though, and Lauren even answered. I told her everything I knew, and she started yelling excitedly, "What do you mean the wedding is off? The wedding can't be off."

"The wedding is off." I thought of our non-refundable tickets, ones we could barely afford in the first place.

"The wedding can't be off. Get out of here!"

"No, it's off. The wedding is off."

"No way the wedding is off!" she yelled, starting to laugh at how ludicrous it was.

"Way!" I yelled back, laughing too.

"I can't believe the fucking wedding is off! This is incredible!"

"The fucking wedding is off," I said.

"Wait," she said, catching her breath, "Dad wants to talk to you."

Dad just had CAT scans and other tests to get everything set up for his whipple operation. He and my stepmother had just returned from Baltimore, where the tests were performed at John Hopkins.

He got on the phone, "I'm a goner."

"What do you mean?"

"I'm a goner. I'm going to die, and there's nothing they can do about it. But I've made my peace with it."

I leapt up from my chair and started pacing back and forth. "What are you talking about? What happened in the test?"

"The cancer is too big, and the tumor is wrapped around a vein. They can't do the surgery. My only concern now is my wife and my kids and grandkids. I've had a good life." He was 63, how could this be happening?

"What are you going to do? Are you having chemo?"

"Oh, yeah, I'll have chemo. There's a chance, 5% or something, that the chemo will shrink the tumor enough to do surgery. Then I can beat this. But I've made my peace with it." My dad had never, as far as I knew, ever made peace with anything; he still held Cadillac-sized grudges against anyone who had ever wronged him, and the list was long and treacherous.

My stepmother quickly took over. "Mel, stop talking that way," she said to him, and then to me, "He's going to do chemo, and he could last for years. He has to stop talking this way and start fighting."

By the time I hung up, I knew we had to go east to see my father. Many phone calls later, we were definitely going. I also started to wonder what was in the air, or the water, in New Jersey where I grew up. It was something

I would wonder about more earnestly over the years, after my mother and aunt both suffered a recurrence of breast cancer, and when five years later, Henry, my stepfather, would also be diagnosed with pancreatic cancer. By that time, there would be articles on the web and in medical journals about the mysterious rise of pancreatic cancer, and far more research linking cancer to environment.

But for now, there was just this deep fear gripping me from the inside, a sense of something far more deadly and extensive than I could let myself think too much about at the moment. Luckily, there was also the immediate need to finish packing.

Do You Recognize Me?

Hurricanes were ripping decks off beach front homes on the TV in my dad's dimly-lit living room where a bunch of us—my son, my step-sister, Wendy, my dad, and me—were engrossed in watching "America's Deadliest Storms." We had just spent an hour sitting on the back deck, my father reaching for my stepmother every time she walked past so he could kiss her, and occasionally saying things like, "This is my last fall," which made Wendy roll her eyes as if he'd told a dirty joke.

Now we were inside, storm-bound, the dinner dishes all washed and just a little time before Ken and I and the kids were to head to Baltimore. A commercial about teeth brightening came on, and everyone but my dad and I slipped off to the kitchen for butter pecan ice cream. The living room was dark, just one lamp on, and I could hear the wind outside, rattling a window behind my head. Rain was coming, probably the rain I had just experienced in Kansas.

My father turned toward me. He had grown thinner, shaved his beard, and his eyes seemed to pop out more than ever behind his thick glasses. He wore a bathrobe, dark and checkered and his feet were bare.

"Do you recognize me?" he asked.

I leaned back in the square floral chair and thought for a moment. "Yeah, I recognize you. I mean, you've lost some weight, but I still recognize you."

His eyes lit up, suddenly burning intensely. "No," he said, "I don't mean the physical. Do you recognize me?" He started to say something about his personality having changed, but I realized very quickly he wasn't talking about personality at all, but something underneath it. He was talking about his soul.

I looked at him, and felt like I was seeing who he was for the first time in a long time, or maybe actually the first time ever. I exhaled and looked very intently into his eyes. "Yeah, I recognize you."

A string of deadly tornados now took our attention back to the screen, where we watched something white and spinning touch down and fill with darkness.

When it was time for our departure, Dad came downstairs from where he'd been napping, wrapped in his bathrobe and wearing his black socks. We first took tons of photos: Dad and the grandkids, Dad and the kids and grandkids, Dad and my stepmother kissing, she and Dad sitting side by side. Finally I went to say goodbye to my father. Usually not a kisser by any stretch, he leaned over and kissed my cheek. Then he leaned over to half-hug Ken, and Ken bent down to kiss him.

"Oh, a guy kissed me!" he joked. "What does that mean?"

"It means you're gay," everyone yelled out, an old family joke.

We loaded the kids into the car and waved goodbye, heading south, right into a massive rainstorm, perhaps not one of America's deadliest, but heavy enough to make the road impressionistic. The three-hour ride to Baltimore took five hours of squinting into the dark, wet sky while driving only 40 mph on interstates. It was the best we could do.

Days later, talking on the phone with Jerry about my conversation with my father, Jerry pointed out, "Yeah, you could have said, 'I finally recognize you.'"

Water

Once again, I sat in the small chemo room, my port hooked up to the IV, and the drugs being carefully administered. I had been given my last big chemo treatment, the whole FAC, a week before, and now I was back for what I hoped was the last of the last, the follow-up 5 Fu. I had a stack of papers with me—congress schedules in the works to revise, a packet from a student to read, and the newspaper in case I had time.

Ken sat across from me, handing me the traditional full Styrofoam cup of ice water. Just the feel of Styrofoam in my hand made me feel nauseous. The highway group had met last night, and we'd decided enough was enough. Besides, continuing to fight the highway department might lose us ground instead of gaining us any. Instead, we would have one of our classic potlucks, where our varied bunch would bring everything from sautéed tofu to Jell-O salad. Now Ken was nudging me to drink the water.

"I've had enough water," I told him as the nurse attached the chemo bag to my slim plastic tubing.

"No, you have to drink it, to wash the chemo out of you."

"I know," I said, bringing the cup to my lips. Cups and cups and cups of water, the best thing I could do each time I received the chemo along with everything else we did—the prayers over each pill and each bag of medicine, the work with Ursula, the rest, the meals brought in from the kitchens of friends all over town, the bad movies we watched, half asleep, with the kids.

In a moment, the chemo was finished, and my port was being rinsed out. In a moment, that was done too.

"Wait here," said Chris, the nurse. I nodded, figuring she had paperwork for me to sign now that I was chemo-done. But when she returned, it was with a greeting card, a balloon and a herd of nurses followed by Dr. Stein.

"Congratulations!" they yelled.

"You're done! You did great! It's all over!"

I hugged each one of them, exclaiming what a surprise it was to have this instant party, this wonderful card they all signed, and then I hugged Dr. Stein too, who giggled a little at the silliness. "Yes, missy, you're all done."

I didn't want to go to the pool. Too much effort. Too far. And being in public in my bathing suit never lifted my spirits. But Natalie persisted.

"Mom, we've hardly been there, and it's going to close soon." She was already wearing a slightly-too-big yellow bikini she inherited from her cousin, and she was stamping her foot.

"We're going to the pool?" said Daniel, rushing to his room to get his suit.

"Forest, get up here now! We're going to the pool!" Natalie yelled down the stairs.

Ken was at a meeting, and it was barely 7 p.m., the end of summer, a summer where I had been around the kids, but not fully present very often. I headed toward my bedroom to get my suit.

We arrived just as the sky was starting to release the heat of the day, the sun behind the trees in the west. While the kids rushed into the water, coming out to stand in line for the slide or try their luck and balance at walking across the lily pad floats in the shallow area, I went to the lap lane.

I hadn't swum in over a year, but I found my way easily to my favorite stroke, the breast stroke, and slowly made my way back and forth, 10 laps before becoming too tired to go on. In doing so, I found the only place in the world, aside from deep sleep, where I felt like a normal, strong, healthy woman. A woman swimming at the speed of very old turtles, but moving on her own accord through another kind of space than ordinary air allowed.

As I swam, I felt the weight of the lush air, moist and still warm, on my face each time I surfaced. On the far side of the fence surrounding the pool, there was a line of majestic pine trees; although they were not native to

Kansas, it seemed like they had lived here long enough to call this home. I breathed in their direction each time I emerged, asking the earth, the air, to help me arrive at whatever ending could be called "healed."

Just the day before, lying on Ursula's table, I had told her that I felt that the chemo has sunk me below the land of the living, or so it felt, and now I was alone and trapped. In fact, I could barely feel the presence of my children at times, of Ken, of my friends. There was only a numbness, and my mind straining to explain what was happening without catching the right note or hue to make sense.

I was poisoning myself to save myself. "Don't cut off your nose to spite your face," my father used to say to me as a child, even if that was exactly what he did all the time with the people closest to him. Wasn't I doing the same with my whole body right now, with willingness and with fear but no real understanding?

"Do you feel your body betrayed you?" Ursula asked as I climbed onto the table.

"No, I don't feel that. I don't feel."

She nodded, and as I closed my eyes, I could feel her hands hovering over my face, and at the same time, a warmth holding my toes, a hand just over my stomach, like a kind of energy healing gymnastics. I felt a tremble behind my eyes, a quiet heavy as rock. But the air holding me was alive.

As I swam, I felt this same air holding the water, holding me, and as I left the bright blue cement of the shore, I hoped I would have the strength to return.

Kissing the Sky

It was near sunset, and the air was cool and bright as Angelica took my hand, and I, in turn, took the hand of the woman next to me. At the bioregional congress, I stood on a ridge in the prairie within this circle of 40 or more women from Mexico, Canada, and the U.S. Wind everywhere, the sky a kind of crystal blue, almost dark and filled with light, the kind of sky that shone most often in early autumn. Angelica, a medicine woman from the Cuernavaca area of Mexico, a grandmother with the face of a female Dalai Lama, encouraged everyone to sing loudly in Spanish, even if we didn't know the words.

Laura, who felt more sister than friend to me, who had come to previous congresses where we had plotted and organized and laughed together about how beautiful all of this work was, held my hand. With her long black curls, her dark eyes like stones at the bottom of a fast river, her curves and swaying skirt, she threw her arms around me. She was here from Cuernavaca and afterwards, her family would stay at our house for most of a week, joining the 20 or so other Mexicans who would also remain in Lawrence after the congress so that we could gather for barbequed tofu and tequila.

On the other side of Laura was Rita, her short gray hair, her eyes shining, her heavy breasts hanging low in her tank top. Joy was there too, tall and looking at me, nodding too. I remembered how, over a decade ago, at a congress in the Ish valley of British Columbia, Joy and I wept in each other's arms at the end of a long ritual led by Starhawk, a Jewish Pagan activist who talked in heavy Brooklynese and led groups in dances and marches like nobody's business.

We sang, and then someone on the end of the circle kissed the person next to her, who passed the kiss on until it reached me, and then I gave Angelica a kiss on her beautiful cheek. She touched her cheek, then her lips, and lifted her hand as she arched her back. We all looked up as she threw the kiss into the big blue sky. As I watched the gesture, I had the feeling that this moment, with an old Mexican healer woman throwing a kiss into the sky, was important for me in ways I couldn't yet understand.

Then she yelled full-throated prayers in Spanish into the air. We all called into the sky, the blueness of it taking our words someplace we couldn't yet see.

Earlier in the congress, 130 of us from Toronto, Mexico City, the Ozarks, New York, San Francisco, and many points in between stood in the big field between our meeting hall and the cabins. Atop a wide mound in the Flint Hills, I once again experienced the sensation of being at high altitude, despite my body still feeling shaky and tired from the last round of chemo two days before.

I looked around the circle to see people I had met two decades before, when my biggest yearning was for Ken to tell me more about how he saw our relationship (he did), and my biggest fear was whether I would ever lose the 10 extra pounds I carried (I didn't). Those decades of congresses were a heady time, meeting in a British Columbia long house to listen to elders from First People nations tell us how their people suffered, or in western Missouri to row to the middle of a lake in a small boat and stay there with many others doing the same thing, so we could listen to the Paul Winter Consort, floating around each other in three rowboats, as they played flute, guitar, didgeridoo, and drums.

Now we were fatter, grayer, our eyes more wizened and our hearts more broken, but we were still listening intently to each other, and trying to learn from one another how to live in community and how to live in greater respect for the land and sky. As usual at the start of all our gatherings, we were going around the circle, asking people to say their names, homes, and passions. I saw Daniel standing between two tall men, trees around him, but when it was his turn, he said loudly, "My passion is to bring together science and the arts, and to help bring down the Bush administration." Applause and laughter.

Out of the corner of my eye, I saw Natalie playing "Red Rover" with a group of kids, all of them running fast across a small stretch of grass near the art building. Forest was sitting near them, reading the latest Harry Potter book. As I returned my attention to the circle, there was Ken, just a dozen people away from me, smiling. He looked more relaxed than I remembered him looking for the last six months. Someone said something to him, and he laughed quietly, caught me watching him, and raised his eyebrows quickly at me.

My vision was like this now, a little wider than before the cancer. I reminded myself often to direct my gaze to the edge of what I could see, take in the tree trembling in the wind I couldn't feel, the child reading on a rock, the man happy in his own skin, the whole circle at once. My sight flooded with love.

On the way back to Lawrence after the congress, I drove with two of the kids and Angelica in the van on a day clear and cooling, the signs of autumn everywhere in the reddening grass and yellowing leaves. Ken was coming later with some others after cleaning up. Angelica spoke almost no English, and I spoke almost no Spanish. I drove, occasionally looking at her and smiling. She was always smiling back.

A flock of birds, large and wide, swept up from the horizon. Around us the grasses, all turning red for the fall, covered all we could see.

"Red," I said, pointing to the grasses.

"Roja," she answered.

We both nodded.

The next night, Ursula and Angelica, neither of whom spoke a language the other knew, sat side by side on the deck at our house. Somehow, they communicated that they would stay in touch in their dreams, supporting each other as only fellow medicine women could.

"How did you make her understand that?" I later asked Ursula. She just shrugged and laughed.

Inside, about two dozen Mexicans, filled our couches and chairs, occasionally breaking into song and often laughing. Joy and Jerry quickly noticed the same thing I did: if we complimented them on anything, a shirt or a bracelet, they immediately took it off and gave it to us. Daniel had earlier told Angelica she had a beautiful woven wallet, and she quickly removed her

U.S. and Mexican money and handed it to him. Taking their cue, we started handing each other earrings and scarves.

"This is the way we were always supposed to live," Joy said, kissing me goodbye as she wore her new (and my old) hummingbird earrings.

Angelica, ready to return to Mexico, had assembled her suitcase and bags around her, and headed toward me with Laura, who, with her husband Fabio and children had bonded like super glue to our family, all of us cleaning the house together, preparing food, and hugging at regular intervals.

"You must stay beautiful," Laura, one of the most gorgeous women any of us knew, said fiercely. "It is up to women to carry the beauty forward."

"It's up to us?" I asked, feeling suddenly very dowdy and lumpy in my worn jeans and old sweater.

"Yes, we are the women. We are the ones who are the holders of beauty in the home, in the congress, on the land, in the world," she answered, smiling widely and lifting her eyebrows.

Angelica said something in Spanish to Laura, and she nodded quickly, then kissed Angelia's cheek before turning back to me.

"My beauty," Laura said, "you are all cured now. Angelica says so." The three of us smiled at each other.

Chapter Seven: Atrophy

Harvest

The flowers that week looked like space aliens, wild orange with tentacles and dark red curls. With Halloween a few days away, there was an elegant bowl of M & M packets beside those flowers, and not the mini size. Ken and I each took one delightedly. We were at Dr. Jew's office, ready to tell her of my decision to have my breasts removed. Even the way it was said by doctors and others we'd talked to about this—"have the breasts removed"—sounded removed to me, as if I were electing to get rid of an unsightly but comfortable couch from the living room.

Once we got to the examining room, Dr. Jew had me, topless of course, lift my arms over my head and make my breasts stand out in various poses. She was happy with her work and my recovery. "Too bad you're going to have to cut away all your good work here," I told her. She shrugged, her black hair pulled into a ponytail, and as usual, she wore a slim strand of pearls.

"You're not going to do reconstruction?" she asked.

"No, it's not for me."

Instead of arguing with me or misunderstanding me, she just nodded, "I didn't think you would do reconstruction. It's not who you are." She leaned on her stool and nodded, her face so young it was hard to believe she was such an experienced surgeon unless, of course, she had started medical school after junior high.

"So," I asked, a little more jauntily, pleased that she understood, "when can you cut off my breasts?"

She half-winced, half-smiled. "Can't you say that in a more positive way?"

"No, I mean, yes, I can say it as a positive in that I'm going to be liberated from the risk of cancer, but it's still a loss."

"Why does it have to be? Why can't you choose to view this as a positive?"

"I see it as a positive, but it's still a negative, I'm still losing part of my sensual body, and I'll have mourning and grieving and whatnot to go through because of that."

She explained how, according to Deepak Chopra who she'd been reading lately, our bodies were changing all the time, every cell recreating itself all the time. "This just blows my mind as a doctor trained in Western medicine," she said enthusiastically, "but I can also see that this could be happening on some level I can't comprehend."

I tried to follow her logic, understand that my body would be evolving, re-creating itself in whole new ways even when my breasts were gone; that this was a beginning, a fresh start, a renewal, a rebirth.

"But it's still a loss," I said.

The gynecological surgeon, Brenda Lofton, was small, energetic, African-American who had a headful of dreadlocks, just returned from Uganda where she served as part of a medical team volunteering their services, she seemed a little out of place in this pastel office clearly tinted to shine with pregnant women and their newborns. One of a bevy of doctors at this office, she shot into the room, shook my hand, and immediately asked me what I did for a living.

"You're a writer? Me, I'm just addicted to books. I can't get anywhere without buying more books. Last week, I went to the bookstore, told myself

I was just looking, even left my purse with my credit card in it in the trunk of the car. But would you believe it? Ten minutes later, I'm racing out to the parking lot to get that credit card. I just can't help myself."

We also talked a lot about what it was like in Uganda.

"People there," she said, as I lay back on the table, my feet in the stirrups, "they need everything. I mean, I just do women here, that's all I do. I haven't examined a man in a million years. And here's this man, he walks in, and drops his pants, and I'm supposed to deal with that?"

I nodded as she put the speculum inside me, looked around, and then slowly pulled it out.

"It's a totally different life there," she said. "We don't know how good we've got it here." I agreed with her as best I could, considering she had half her hand in my vagina, which she was studying intently.

Of course, we also talked a lot about the removal of my ovaries, and whether the cervix and uterus should come along for the trip. At first, she explained that certainly they should because otherwise the vagina could atrophy, a thought that obviously scared me. Yet she was willing to leave the uterus or take it, whatever I wanted.

"And what about the breasts? You want to do reconstruction?"

"No."

She nodded, tilted her head, so I said more, but since I was in a wise-ass mood, I told her, "I don't want to collude with the patriarchy."

She didn't blink. "Okay, but I want you to get a sonogram just to make sure I'm not going to have any surprises when I get inside you." She also had her nurse test me, immediately, for ovarian cancer with the CA-125 blood test, a test with a reputation for being inaccurate but still somewhat helpful.

I nodded, and went home with Ken, driving the long way through some back roads while we listened to a call-in radio show about Thanksgiving cooking. Apparently, this man in Georgia deboned every kind of poultry imaginable and then put them all together—a Cornish hen inside a chicken inside a duck inside a turkey. It took him weeks, and he had to keep the meat half-frozen the whole time to keep it from going bad.

"Do you think your feat is a little unusual?" the radio host asked, obviously raising his eyebrows.

"Well, maybe for some people, but for me, it's a form of relaxation."

Thanksgiving

The turkey was the least of it. Frozen way beyond our plans for it, it took an extra hour and a half to cook. Meanwhile, there was a Chinese stir-fry, some marinated green beans, the most incredibly buttery mashed potatoes in the world, sweet potatoes half covered (to please my father-in-law) with mini-marshmallows, a few huge salads, too many pies and cakes, and various side dishes vying for our attention. The people poured in quickly: Ken's parents; his sister, brother-in-law, and their three adopted girls from India; a Chinese friend and her mother, who didn't speak English, but loved to smile and sew; Judy and her husband, Stan; and our friends, Steve and Jeannette.

Most everyone stayed in or near the kitchen heating and reheating, stirring and mixing, washing and piling during the time we waited for the turkey to make its debut. The Chinese grandmother took over ironing the tablecloth, on the table, all the time smiling and saying something to the effect that we were a nice, if disorganized, family. My Indian nieces helped her lay out the tablecloth, and adjust it in order to iron each edge.

After dinner, all the kids ran off to watch movies, the men went outside to watch the sky through several telescopes, the Chinese people and Ken's parents went home, and the women still among us stayed in the kitchen, visiting together on folding chairs rented for the occasion. I told them my new concerns about vaginal atrophy.

"Hey, it's real, believe me," said Jeannette. "When you get older, it's amazing what happens to parts of you."

"Penises too," said Judy. "I hear they atrophy also."

"How would you know?" I asked

"Well, one thing we could do is all go home, measure our husband's penises, and then measure again in ten years, see if there's any difference," said Jeanette.

"Yeah, and they'll all say that we better use yardsticks to measure them," added Judy. We started laughing so hard that we decided to have more pie to calm us down.

That night, I called my father to wish him a happy Thanksgiving.

"Wait," he said, having just woken from a nap. My stepmother told me he was sleeping all the time now, so I was surprised he answered. "I can't hear you."

"I'M CALLING TO WISH YOU A HAPPY THANKSGIVING!"

"Yeah, Thanksgiving. We had all the usual," he said, and I knew that meant my Italian stepmother had laid out lasagna in a tray large enough to rival any turkey, with turkey too, meatballs and sausages, antipasto, mashed potatoes, and pie.

"That's great," I said.

"I can't hear you. Why don't you call me back?"

I hung up and dialed again. He answered, "Wait, I can't hear you, call me back again."

I hung up and called him again. "Hello, Dad?"

"I still can't hear you. Call me back again."

I hung up and dialed again. This time, both he and my stepmother answered on different phones, and each, thinking the call was for the other, promptly hung up when I said hello.

I called again. "I still can't hear you. What's your number? I'll call you back," he said. I gave him my number and hung up. And waited. And waited some more.

Five more minutes, and I called him back. He was sleeping now, said my stepmother, and not up to talking on the phone.

Vacuums and Joysticks

"Oophorectomy is a funny word, but I'm learning to say it lately," my mother confessed to me on the phone, referring to the sucking out of my ovaries. They would first be loosened and cut free of their attachments, then removed with a vacuum cleaner instrument the size of a toothbrush, I supposed, and it would all be over. All this and the double mastectomy would be done together on a February morning.

"Yeah, it's a really strange word," I told her, as I searched for my purse and then fished out my car keys. I had the ovarian sonogram scheduled today, certain it would show nothing, considering how healthy my reproductive organs had proved themselves to be, churning out babies, generally doing all I ever expected of them. Then again, I had once felt the same way about my breasts, which turned out to have a secret past.

"Are you sure you're okay going alone?" she asked.

"Sure, I mean, it's just routine." But even as I said this, I started to have doubts. I swept them from my mind and drove into Kansas City listening to music, singing along, happy that soon I would be done with all these kinds of visits. The land seemed flatter, losing its green quickly this fall. Dr. Lofton's waiting room was full of soft pinks and blues, gentle lighting, and the company of very pregnant women and their toddling babes in arms. All the magazines focused on the delivery and sustenance of babies.

Once called and accounted for, I was led to a small room normally used to show expectant moms their fetuses. The ceiling was covered with glow-in-the-dark stars "for the kids who come along with their moms," the technician explained. She was friendly and seemed competent as she told me to strip from my waist down, but to keep my socks. Then she would do the sonogram and we would see my ovaries on the screen. I nodded and did as she said.

When she began the procedure, she was chatting with me amicably about her family's plans for Christmas. She told me right away that my uterine wall was preparing to shed itself, and I would soon have a period, something I had suspected because of those long-forgotten but easily-remembered cramps and moodiness of late.

I was explaining to her about our Hanukkah plans when she fell abruptly silent, and kept pressing on my left side, staring at the screen intently. I started to study the stars on the ceiling, wondering how brightly they would light up when it was darker in this room.

"What is it?" I asked after a few minutes.

"I think there's a cyst here."

"Why would that be? Could it be related to just having finished chemo?" I had read that sudden changes in hormone levels could create cysts, something common to many women, but with cancer beating its drums so loud in my mind at this moment, I felt more than a little nervous.

"Perhaps." She told me she would have to do a vaginal sonogram. What this turned out to be was a giant joystick of sorts inserted into me that she twisted around and probed for what seemed like hours, but probably only for about ten minutes.

I tried to lie still, tried to act like it was okay for me to have this giant plastic probe, the thickness of a healthy cucumber, inside me, making the rounds. I tried to get her to tell me more.

"This cyst, is it on the left side or the right?" I figured it was probably nothing, just a little blip.

"Both."

I started to panic. "That's serious, isn't it?"

"I can't say. Your doctor will have to discuss this with you." She continued manipulating the joystick, pausing to snap pictures while the machine beside me shot out a long line of photos of various angles of my insides. She can't say, I told myself, so it must be serious.

She pulled out the device, told me to get dressed, and said the doctor would see me soon, promising me a very short wait in the waiting room. I got dressed, starting to tremble. Ovarian cancer, how could this be? I obediently went to the waiting room where I spent not a few minutes, as I expected, but a whole hour surrounded by howling babies, strutting pregnant women, and baby magazine advertisements for strollers and bottles.

Wasn't breast cancer enough? Wasn't it enough to have lymph nodes involved and to go through chemo for so long? Wasn't losing my breasts enough? Wasn't my dad being terminally ill at 63 enough? How dare this happen! To top it off, some toddler twins, screaming in the next bevy of chairs, kept distracting me from freaking out even more.

When I finally got to Dr. Lofton's examining room, I could hardly contain myself. I let the nurse take my blood pressure, temperature, other vitals, all the while shaking a little. Finally, Dr. Lofton walked in, frowning and carrying a pile of photos of my ovaries in one hand, and a box of tissues in the other. This couldn't be a good sign.

"I'm not going to lie to you," she said, sitting on the stool across from me, "I don't like the looks of this—bilateral cysts, but at least they're small, only about three centimeters each."

Those dimensions, compared to what I knew of breast cancer tumor size, seemed gigantic.

"And you're not going to like what I'm going to say, but laparoscopic surgery is out of the question right now, and so is keeping your uterus. We're going to have to cut you open, mid-line incision, and take everything. Now this probably isn't anything serious, but just in case it is, we need to cut you this way so, if we have to, we can do ovarian cancer staging."

Ovarian cancer. A real possibility. Although I had held it together with every other doctor through all the other bad news, this time I felt myself coming apart at the seams. A killer cancer, and it could be in me. My voice started shaking as I spoke, and before I knew it, I was out-and-out crying. "It's just that I've been though so much already. I can't do this also."

Dr. Lofton nonchalantly handed me a tissue. "I know, I know. And it's probably going to be benign, but just to make sure, we've got to do this surgery and see what's happening. There's really no other way to do an accurate biopsy."

"But my CA-125 was normal, right?"

"Yeah, your CA-125 was 10, and I've never seen a woman with a normal CA-125 have ovarian cancer, but I have seen some with CA-125s in the hundreds be just fine." She paused. "Still, you never know until you know."

"I think we need to do the surgery sooner rather than later," I said, immediately counting the days and figuring if we could do it within a week or so, I could still go to my Vermont residency in seven weeks.

"I completely agree, and we're going to make it happen. I'll have my scheduling person set something up."

"Before next week, right?"

"One way or another."

I half-hugged her, and left the office, dialing my cell phone on my way down to the parking lot. Everyone was completely supportive although a little scared, too. Ken told me we would get through this. Margo, from Goddard, said we would work out a way for me to handle the residency from home, perhaps meeting with my group via phone conferences, and she would step in whenever and however needed. I was relieved and panicked at once, all the way back to town where I met Judy at a coffee shop. We sat across from each other, and she stared into my eyes, completely supportive, just the way she had been all through the chemo treatments and surgery before.

"How am I supposed to sit with this one?" I asked. I remembered that after the car accident Judy told me, "Whatever happens, you'll deal with it." At the time, I said, "No, some things I'll never be able to deal with."

This time, she just reached out her hand and held mine. We both tried not to cry.

That night, I tried to stir-fry chicken and vegetables, but I felt too edgy, and kept slamming the pan on the stove, yelling at the kids, and feeling like I was going to scream for hours. I couldn't tell them what was happening, that their mother who had been through so much might now be facing further ordeals.

"Can I have a hamburger?" Forest asked.

"No, just eat your spaghetti."

"But there's no cheese."

"Just eat it!"

There was no place to go but here, and here was the last place I wanted to be.

Later that night, Natalie sidled into my bedroom. She looked worried, although I hadn't told her anything; I was just getting absorbed in the latest issue of *People* so I could avoid reality. She closed the door behind her.

"What's up?" I asked. She sat on the edge of my bed, her brown eyes intent on something. Could she know? Could she have simply felt it from the distance I kept from the kids at this moment?

"I don't know. I'm just having a depression."

I paused in my reading, tried to think of what to say, but nothing would come except, "Well, that sucks."

"Yeah, it does," she said.

Smart Women

I was sitting in Papa Keno's over giant slices of pizza with the kids and Ken, chatting speedily on the cell phone with Dr. Lofton, who was telling me about her own hysterectomy. She had called me about whether to schedule the hysterectomy at the same time as the mastectomy, which, at first, she and I thought would be a great idea, but now she had doubts, remembering her own experience. "Could you walk afterwards pretty soon?" I asked.

"Hey, we'll get you up and walking that day if possible, but when I had mine, I didn't have any idea just how much it would hurt afterwards." I nodded into the phone.

Ken put a giant slice of pizza in front of me, and I started sprinkling on parmesan cheese.

Forest and Daniel were each reading their own issue of a local entertainment newspaper while Natalie arranged just the right amount of parmesan on each part of her pizza. They wanted to go to the library after dinner, where the high speed internet thrilled them.

"It really hurts?"

"You're not going to believe how much it hurts," she said.

I called my father that night. Luckily, he was awake, a rarity now that he was sleeping something like 20 hours a day. ("Like a cat," Ken told me.) I talked to him about his next doctor appointment, and then broke the news. "It looks like there's something going on in my ovaries," I said loud and clear. Ovaries. What would I be talking about next? "I'm going to need to have a hysterectomy right away just to make sure. But they don't think it's serious."

He took it in, told me to speak to my stepmother, that she could tell him about it again later, but he needed to get some sleep right now.

A day or so later, I came home to find Dr. Jew's voice on my answering machine, saying, "I need to talk with you, and you're going to be disappointed." There was a number for me to call, and though I punched the buttons of the phone furiously, I knew I had missed her.

"What could it be?" I asked Ken. We mulled over all the possibilities that night while passing the toothpaste. Perhaps she didn't want Ursula in the operating room after all, or maybe her schedule wasn't going to work out like we thought it would.

"Yeah, it must be Ursula," I concluded. "It must be that the hospital has some new policy or something against energy healers in the operating room." We finished brushing our teeth in agreement.

Then next day at the coffee shop, my cell phone rang, and it was Dr. Jew.

She and Dr. Lofton had discussed whether doing the double mastectomy and hysterectomy together was too much for my body. My torso, she reminded me, would be cut apart vertically below the belly, horizontally above the waist. The two doctors had concluded that it was too much for someone just finishing chemo.

I argued with her. Why couldn't we just do it? Why couldn't I just be done with all of this? I was strong enough, I could take it, it would be okay, and all the other doctors acted like it would be okay, too.

"None of the other doctors talked to me before they told you that," she answered, then softened her tone, "I'm just looking out for what's best for you."

I hung up the little phone. I was furious at Dr. Jew, furious at the other doctors, and furious that I would have months more of this waiting and planning, my body incomplete between one surgery and another. I walked out of the coffee shop and headed over to the school to pick up Natalie and Forest, and then drove Natalie to her piano lesson.

As I was driving back to the piano studio to get Natalie and then hit the supermarket to let the kids pick out something for dinner that I wouldn't have to cook, Dr. Lofton rung me up. I had calmed down considerably, even though Natalie was arguing with me about why we couldn't just have pizza for the fourth night in a row. I told her to be quiet while I answered the phone.

"Yeah, I thought I'd give you some time to cool down from Dr. Jew's news before I called," she said.

"You're a smart woman," I told her. "And tell Dr. Jew I'm sorry I got so upset, and that I'm on board with this and I understand it's the best for me. It was just hard to accept that this will go on for months more."

"It's always hard to accept things like this. Believe me, I'm with you." I thanked her, made jokes about how crazy I felt lately, and went shopping.

A few nights later, Ken and I were sitting in the bedroom as I went over plans for surgery, the likelihood that the cysts would be nothing, and other reassuring words to keep the real fear at bay. Ken said nothing, just sat on the floor and leaned against the bed with an open book in his lap, looking like someone I had just spied at a library, but had never actually met.

"How come you're not saying anything?" I asked.

He shrugged. "I guess I'm just tired." He barely looked up from the book.

Daniel rushed in. "Natalie is being a jerk, and I want you to do something about it right now."

"Not now, Daniel, I'm talking to your dad."

"No, I can't wait. She said I could have the computer at 8:00, and it's past eight, and she won't stop playing her stupid Sims game."

"Okay, go get your sister," I said, figuring his trek to the basement and back would give us some time. "And close the door," I yelled after him.

I turned back to Ken. "You haven't said anything for days. What's going on?"

He opened his eyes wider, the blue in the centers of each around the pupil now feathering to green, and looked carefully at me. A long time passed, him on the floor, looking up at me on the worn-out recliner inherited from his parents that recently replaced the one we found on a curb.

"What?" I asked again.

"It's too much," he replied.

"What's too much?"

Natalie jerked open the door. "It's my turn, and it's still my turn because he traded me some computer time to watch that stupid movie about gravity."

"I did not. That was Forest," yelled Daniel.

"Shut up," she yelled back.

"You shut up."

"Both of you shut up, and stop saying 'shut up,'" I said.

Ken rolled his eyes and went back to his book until Natalie elbowed Daniel, and he pushed her.

"Okay, both of you to your rooms," said Ken, looking up again.

"And stay there!" I yelled.

Finally, they left, and I turned back to Ken. "What's too much?"

He didn't look up.

"Please, what is too much?"

Forest opened the door. "Dad, could you tuck me in?"

"You're not even in your pajamas," I told him, although pajamas for him simply meant taking off everything but his underwear.

Another 10 minutes passed, during which time all three kids had a fight over brushing their teeth, Ken tucked Forest in, and Natalie pulled me into her room to air her list of complaints against both brothers. I hugged her, said something about how hard it was being the girl in the middle, and feeling a bit grateful that I was one of three sisters who'd surrounded one brother.

Finally, we came back to our perches in the bedroom.

"So what is too much?" I asked again, irritation rushing into my face.

"This," he answered, "is just too much for me. I can't deal with it."

"What do you mean you can't deal with it? We have to deal with it. It's not like a choice."

He looked at the rug, badly in need of replacement, and then looked up slowly at me. "It's too much," he said. "I can't." His eyes were red, and he looked utterly exhausted.

Waiting Rooms of Hell

I've heard the analogy that hell is a series of waiting rooms, each one getting smaller and smaller. I'm sure they're located at some kind of medical clinic.

The visit to Dr. Julia Chapman, the gynecological oncologist who was to assist in my hysterectomy, brought Ken and me to the University of Kansas Medical Center on a brilliant winter day. The process of finding her through a maze of spaces and what seemed like various time zones was anything but brilliant, much like how lost I felt whenever I tried to reason with myself about the surgery. It was going to happen soon, anyway, but now just a little sooner. I would get to lie in bed and read a lot of good books. People would feed me, the staples would come out in a week or so, I would walk into the cold, open field and feel great joy at being alive. There would be flowers and candles, strong painkillers and warm quilts.

Yet something in me was unconvinced, no matter how I deconstructed every aspect of the surgery. "You sure it's not cancer?" I asked Ken for the 32nd time.

"Yes," he said, as we drove through one diversion, then another, trying to negotiate the center's four-story parking garage. Underneath this question, under the surface words about the details of surgery, there was something stirring like ice in the center of my body, telling me I was downright afraid. Up, up, up to the top of the parking garage we went, finding every slot filled. As we rounded corners I stared at the parking lot ceiling, which was way too low for my comfort. Finally, we reached the open sky again on the top floor, where parking spots abounded.

"I like being on the top," I told Ken as I flung myself into my coat while climbing out of the car.

"I know," he said.

We both giggled and headed toward the stairwell where we went down flight after flight, far more than seemed possible. Eventually we made our way into the cancer center, where we were seated in a crowded waiting room. I picked up a magazine and started turning the pages nervously past Martha Stewart's financial mess and Trent Lott's political mess. Out of the corner of my eye, I saw Santa Claus leaving chemo treatment: an old man with the perfect beard, mustache, requisite white hair and big belly, and even a Santa Claus hat.

"Look, Santa's leaving." I nudged Ken. "Even he has cancer." But he just glanced up quickly, then back to his newspaper with not so much as an "uh huh." The television blared something about a car accident and a neighborhood response, and an old woman beside me dressed in purple polyester refused, when asked by a nurse, to say which of the two receptionists she liked best, the large gay man with slicked back hair or the petite African-American woman surrounded by poinsettias. "You're not going to get me caught in that one," the old woman said. "I love them both." She, along with many others surrounding me, was a regular, which meant regular hugs from various staff people sporting Christmas wreath pins.

Finally, our names were called along with several others, and we were led in a parade down a series of halls. The old woman in purple was just ahead of me, clutching the arm of the nurse.

"What's your name, honey?" she asked.

"Oh, you know me. I'm Louise," the nurse said as she held the woman's hand tightly, leading her steadily toward her chemo treatment.

"I do? Well, it's good to meet you again."

We were led into a much smaller waiting room, this one playing "Days of Our Lives" on the TV set as Ken and I rooted through *National Geographic* and *Vanity Fairs*. I looked at photos of a woman living with gorillas while on screen the district attorney (who was somehow related to the prosecuting attorney) told the judge, "I have to come forth because the man I charged isn't the one who killed Gloria Teasdale. It was someone right in this courtroom." Everyone in the courtroom gasped as I turned to an article about a villa in Tuscany where the stars love to sunbathe and read their scripts.

We stayed in this room for almost an hour, glancing up hopefully every time the nurse came round. Eventually she called my name again, and we were led to an even smaller room, where we sat, me on an examining table, Ken in the only chair, and waited for another 20 minutes. There wasn't much to say except, "How long have we been here?" and "Wish I'd brought in some of the magazines." But we kept talking, trying to explain to ourselves what was happening.

Then a resident entered, introduced herself, and sat down on the stool, pen and chart in hand. "Now can you tell me why you believe you're here right now?" she asked.

I was tired and a little nervous, and this question seemed a bit unnecessary, but I went into what I knew about the cysts, needing this surgery, how Dr. Chapman was asked to be on-call, but she preferred to assist in such cases, and she wanted to meet with patients before she operated, so here I was.

The resident, with her curled-under, thick blond hair, seemed pleasant enough. She started asking me the same questions I had answered everywhere else. How many children? How many pregnancies? Any sexually-transmitted diseases? Age at first period? Date of last period? Any pain or discomfort?

As soon as the door closed, Ken and I looked at each other. "Hey, did I tell you I spoke to my dad yesterday?" I asked him. "He actually asked me how my poetry was going. He's never asked me about my poetry before."

"Dying is changing him."

"Yeah, he was great. He was so supportive of me and all the kids and everything. It's like I finally have the father I always wanted." Ken nodded, and we looked around the room.

"That painting is all wrong," Ken said of a landscape with the moon setting over a patterned lake and a beautiful balcony full of plants. "The shadows are going the wrong way for morning, and the moon would only be setting like that in the morning."

"I hate that poster of the happy and sad faces and level of pain each feels."

"Got a pen? You could add mustaches."

I leapt up and over to the poster, which was taped to a bathroom door. I immediately drew a few mustaches, then we heard someone enter the bathroom from the corridor, and I raced back to my perch on the table.

"You could add glasses too, and how about some piercings?"

"This pen doesn't write so well sideways," I told him, but I snuck back over and gave the mild-pain guy gladiator glasses, and the no-pain man some wire rim ones. I was about to pierce the nose of the happy one when we heard some shuffling out in the hall, and I shot back to my seat again.

Dr. Chapman was dressed casually in a sweater and checkered pants. She smiled immediately and entered the room with an air of someone who knew exactly where she was and what she was doing, shaking my hand as if we were meeting at a fabulous lawn party on the Cape.

"You're the doctor?" I asked incredulously. Somehow, all the waiting made everything now seem oddly anticlimactic. The doctor nodded, and immediately began talking to me about the surgery.

"Yes, I am," she answered quickly. She was probably used to being asked this question, because she looked far younger than she was. "This," she said, immediately shifting to my ovarian cyst, "is probably benign. In fact, if you didn't have the BRCA mutation, we wouldn't even worry about surgery right away."

"What makes you think it's benign? My low score on the CA-125 test?"

"That test has about a 50% false negative rate, so I never go by the test alone. But as soon as I saw you, I could see you were healthy. You don't have

146

any symptoms, and you're having regular periods. Those are good signs in my book." She slid her stool back against the wall so she could rest her back.

She launched into some fast talk about various studies, the reliability of various results, and the various staging procedures if the cyst did turn out to be cancerous. I began to sense that she was a female counterpart of Dr. Stein: clear, well-researched, caring, awake, able to plunge into any detail with amazing precision.

I asked her my questions about the procedure, recovery time, when the staples would come out, what exactly would be done if cancer was found, going through the list several times for reassurance that she really thought the cysts were benign. That reassurance was needed all the more after she explained how ovarian cancer staging was done. The lymph nodes were removed, she showed me, doing a quick drawing of some tunnels and circles that represented, on pink patient chart paper, my reproductive system. Then, she would remove the oventum, a fatty girdle that hung down and basically did nothing important. I imagined a frilly curtain hanging somewhere in the pelvic cavity to keep the sun from shining in too brightly. Other things would be snipped and slid out through the incision between my pelvic bone and belly button, which could be extended to my breast bone if need be.

"But if it was ovarian cancer, it would be caught very early, wouldn't it?"

"Oh, yes, and with most stage one and stage two ovarian cancers, no chemotherapy is needed after surgery." I asked her a little about the chemotherapy, pointing out that I had just ingested plenty of cytoxen and adriomyicen, two of the best agents in the past for treating ovarian cancer.

"But they only work well in conjunction with platinum. That's the best chemotherapy we have for ovarian cancer, and without it, the tumors will grow right through the cytoxen and adriomyicen." My heart sank just a little as we went on to talk about how hard it was to go through ovarian cancer chemo, "much more difficult than treating breast cancer," she told me.

"And you really think what I have is benign?" I asked once more.

She stood up to leave and shook my hand. "Some women elect to keep their ovaries when they're BRCA positive. I understand that the surgical procedure is only one part of dealing with a much bigger issue. There's also the psychological components. This is a big change," she added, putting her hand on my shoulder.

I nodded, we glanced at Ken's watch, and then zoomed out of there to drive back to Lawrence, 20 minutes late to pick up the kids from school. All the way home, we listened to singer-songwriter Greg Greenway sing about desire, courage, love, pain, loss, the CD blaring as we shot through miles of a winter-faded landscape. The waiting seemed to travel with us: waiting for surgery, waiting for pathology reports, waiting fervently to receive anything but bad news.

Face-Down on the Earth

In Ursula's small, bright office, I sat in the chair opposite her, trying to explain myself. I had used the phrase, "I don't know" an embarrassing number of times, and I realized that I wasn't really feeling anything—a keep-it-quiet-or-you'll-wake-the-baby attitude permeated most of my emotions.

I looked over toward Ursula and said, "I don't know if it's the possibility of ovarian cancer, or the fact that they're going to be cutting me open, or just losing my uterus and all those other organs. I mean, everything seems so healthy, and it doesn't make sense to me that I'm going to get them all yanked out." I felt like my organs were, in the paranoid world of the cancer patient, guilty until proven innocent.

She nodded and pointed at the table.

Once lying down, I thought of my uterus, my cervix, my ovaries, all of which had worked so well, serving me as I got pregnant quickly and easily, growing babies miraculously, and even more miraculous, pushing those babies, impossible as it seems now, through that small opening out into the big world. I had done it all at a free-standing birthing center without drugs (although in the midst of labor, had drugs been available, I would've knocked off armies of nuns to get to them). Then, I had nursed all these babies with hardly an infection and with plenty of milk. During each stretch of pregnancy or nursing, I mused often that my short, somewhat overweight, low-to-the-ground, wide-hipped, and soft-bellied body seemed custom-made for incubating, birthing, and feeding babies. Whatever my flaws were according to the standards of feminine beauty, they actually came in handy when it came to motherhood.

I knew from talking with Ursula that parts of the body that were cut away actually remained there in the energetic field, which did a lot to explain the phantom pain experienced by amputees. Even if my womb and all its appliances, an inner kitchen of new life, were removed, all would still be with me in some shadowy way.

That afternoon, I went down to the prairie in the valley below our house. It was cold, but bearable, as I lay face down on the ground, the sun warming my back, and the wind only slightly brushing its chill over me. I felt my stomach on the earth, the ground supporting me, even cradling me with its thick cover of fallen-over prairie grass. It was far more comfortable than I imagined, the ground soft and hard at once. What was shifting in me and around me as I was held?

I didn't know, but I loved the feeling of the grass cushioning my curves and shallows. Ken had explained to me that the earth often became softer in winter as the dirt filled with air. The earth inhales.

Many years ago, at another bioregional congress, Starhawk, who was leading a women's ceremony, asked us to lie face down on the earth and speak, sing, cry, or whisper into the ground whatever grief we carried. "Okay, whatever," I thought, the sarcastic teenager in my head rolling her eyes, but when I lay on the earth that warm afternoon, my body automatically shuddered, and I found myself crying into the grass, my forehead trembling on the earth. I couldn't name the grief of that moment, but it happened less than a week before I got pregnant with Daniel, as I stood on the cusp between woman and mother. My breasts and uterus at the time were ready to give themselves over to a life I couldn't imagine until I was living it.

Today, turning my head to the other side and coming face to face with the reddening stems of big bluestem, I was lost in a forest of grass. I remembered David Wagoner's poem, "Lost," in which he writes, "You are surely lost. Stand still. The forest knows/ Where you are. You must let it find you." The grasses found me, the blue of the sky dimming violet in the distance. The wind found me, galloping across my back as if I were just another crested wave in the field.

Never mind that it was December, that this afternoon was not particularly warm, that the sun was close to the ledge of the horizon. I was warm enough.

"You're not going to need any champagne this New Year's eve because you'll be tripped up on morphine," Denise said the day before surgery.

"Yeah, you'll get all the good drugs," Courtney added.

"Woo hoo," I answered, which made them laugh. We went back to finalizing the plans about when they would pick up each kid from school, take them to the hospital then back home, where they would stay with the kids until my mother and Henry arrived for the night. As usual, a team of people—nearly impossible now to distinguish whether its members were friends or family, because everyone had turned into both—had gathered around, flying in and driving in, willing to do whatever we asked. I was especially thankful to my mother and Henry for flying in once again to ferry kids wherever they needed to go.

"You guys," I said as they were getting ready to leave the house. "I don't know what we'd do without you."

"You just take care of yourself," my mother said.

"Hey, we love you, Lassman family, just remember that," Denise said, hugging Ken, and then me. "Even if there's going to be a little less of you," she added.

Champagne and celebration were alien ideas when I awoke from surgery on the last day of the year. I didn't feel any pain, just a vast quiet; a gentle place except for one terrible fact: I was itchy all over.

"Oh, lots of people get itchy on morphine," one of the nurses told me.

But my itchiness increased vehemently over the next few hours as I slept and woke until, around 2 a.m., I begged the nurses to stop the morphine drip. Whatever the pain was, it had to be easier to deal with than feeling like the inside of my skin was crawling all over itself.

Meanwhile, there were faces around me when I woke between the long drifts of sleep. I saw Suzanne, an old, dear friend visiting from Vermont, who woke me up and then said, "Go to sleep, just go back to sleep." There was Laurie, moving around the room, asking if I needed anything. Jerry looked into my eyes and mildly smiled. Ken held my hand, and moved some of my clothes into the little closet. I knew exactly where I was and what had happened, but the room was made of shifting clouds and quiet, voices telling me I was fine.

There was also the news, repeated by everyone: when the surgeon got into my ovaries, there was nothing there, not even cysts.

All this happened to the whoosh-whoosh of the enormous power booties they'd put on my doggies—bright blue, pumping booties that squeezed my feet with all their might and then let go, one foot at a time. I felt like I was horizontally climbing mountains in the snow. I knew I had to wear them to jump-start my circulation, but I hated those booties, and by morning I had wiggled out of them and refused to put them back on for more than a minute or two.

I shifted my attention to the television, which told me how Ryan O'Neill's drug-addicted kids kept screwing up their lives. Then came the weather channel (when Ken had the remote), the musical *South Pacific* with Mitzi Gaynor washing that man right out of her hair (when I had the remote), the weather channel again, then a whirl of detective shows I kept skimming past.

Gradually, my mind woke up enough to know what time it was, and my body woke enough to feel a little, and then a lot, of pain. Sitting up, even with the push-button ease of the electric bed, was excruciating. Standing, after the first day, was agony. Walking was downright heroic.

On the second day, I made it to the plastic recliner chair where Ken piled blankets on me and I sat very still, trying to spoon the beef broth into my mouth before I moved on to the excitement of red Jell-O, which, after surgery, tasted like nirvana. That was when the mob paraded in: my kids, my mom and Henry, Ken's folks, and his sister and brother-in-law, packing the little hospital room, sitting and leaning wherever they could.

I wasn't used to seeing them all together and in this context, and it was hard to know what to talk about, so conversation quickly dove to the lowest common denominator. "She's sitting up now by herself," Ken said. I felt like a three-month-old.

"Yeah, that's great. You look great, Caryn," someone said.

My kids hung back, a little shy to see their mom so quiet and bundled up and having just gone through some kind of incomprehensible thing they would learn more about when they got older.

There was some joking about a football game, some talk about finding the hospital, and then, thankfully, Dr. Lofton walked in. Well, actually, first she had to get the door open, which took a little people-rearranging, and then she had to survey the whole room.

"Hi, Dr. Lofton," I offered. "So good to see you. This is my daughter, Natalie, and my sons, Daniel and Forest, and that's Ken's mom, and that's my sister-in-law... ."

It took a while to introduce everyone as she nodded, a little incredulous to see me with a cast of thousands.

Within a few seconds, it was just her and Ken and me.

"You need to rest. You can't have all these people here right now."

"Yeah, tell me about it," I answered.

"Fifteen minutes, and then they've got to go," she added.

I was extremely relieved, feeling more keenly that the staples in my stomach were pulling on me, the internal walls severed and reattached, the tubes running up me and down me, pulling and pumping. I slowly unswaddled myself and lifted my nightgown. She removed the tape and lifted away the gauze. I watched intently, seeing a long, slightly crooked line of staples holding me together, my stomach truly split open and not yet very good at closing itself back together. There was blood everywhere, and my skin was soft and swollen, kind of like a mass of pizza dough with black marker ink and catsup spread all over it. It looked like a nightmare made of flesh.

"This looks beautiful," she exclaimed. "You're healing beautifully."

"You think?"

"Yes, this looks great. And you heard the lab report, didn't you?" she said, looking up at my face now. "Nothing, completely clear, even the cysts were gone."

"But they weren't the type that were supposed to go away on their own, were they?"

"No, but they sure did."

I felt great relief but also confusion. Why I had I undergone this surgery now and in this way if I didn't have those cysts? Why did my body have to be split apart this way at this time? She went on to tell me how good it was to visit with Dr. Chapman, sharing stories about their less fortunate patients as they cut and sewed me up, enjoying a chance to have some doctor time together. "And you looked so good that you never have to worry about us talking about you when we're working on a more fortunate patient."

By the time the doctor left and the nurse came back to pull out my catheter and disconnect me from the IV now that I was cleared for lift-off into solid foods, I had devised a plan to deal with the tottering mob outside my room.

"Could you," I asked this nurse, who was using her large and fumbling hands to try to wrap my naked hips in a girdle thing that would give me a little more support, "tell everyone out there that the doctor said I needed to go back to sleep?"

"Oh, hon, of course I will, and I'm so glad you thought of that on your own."

It wasn't hard; I was exhausted and wanting to submerge myself back into total unconsciousness for as long as I could. Days later, back in my own recliner in my own room, my mother sat down on my bed opposite me. "You told that nurse to kick us out," she said, laughing.

"How did you know?"

"I'm your mother, of course I could tell."

"Well, I was so tired, and there were just too many of you." We laughed until we finally moved on to plans for her to fetch dinner, as she did so often during her time here.

Days later, I walked to the mailbox with Forest. It was about 40 degrees and sunny outside, and it was a long walk from the front door to the mailbox. "About three city blocks," I, the native Brooklyner, would explain to people visiting for the first time. I felt every block as I carefully stepped down the rocky driveway with Forest, who had refused to wear a coat and was a little red-eared from the mild wind.

He held my hand the whole way. His hands were those of a builder or a healer; they were large, and when he held my hand, I always felt warmth crossing from him to me. We smiled and didn't say much on the way there.

After successfully mounting the hill and following it down to the mailbox, where I retrieved a few more beautiful get-well cards, we started heading back, still holding hands.

"When you don't have cancer anymore, can we go to Worlds of Fun?" he asked.

"I don't have cancer anymore. But it's winter, and Worlds of Fun is closed. Besides, I'm still recovering."

"Oh," he said.

"Do you want to see the scar?" I asked him.

He nodded. I lifted the elastic band from my waist and pulled it down enough to show him the row of neat staples following the still slightly crooked line from belly button on down. He flinched. "It's okay," I said. "It doesn't hurt anymore." He nodded, and took my hand again, holding it all the way home.

Chapter Eight:
The New Land

Spirit Trip

The sky was tinged pink, and so was the snow bordering the sunset as we drove to the airport, just Ken and me heading for Pittsburgh, and then the small town in central Pennsylvania where my father was dying. He had fallen into a semi-comatose state a week and a half earlier, when flying was still strictly out of the question for me. But he'd hung on, and now here he was, still alive, so I had booked us tickets, a rental car, hotel rooms, the whole works, by recklessly bidding low (and winning) each time on an internet travel site.

The light grew pinker as we drove into the blue eastern horizon. We didn't know if we would find him dead or alive, or how we'd find the rest of the family, surely exhausted by close calls when his breath would slow and they'd wait by his bed, trying to make sure he wouldn't die alone. Although my incision was healed shut, I still felt a little worn down, hovering just under the surface of being able to function like a regular person again. When I had asked Dr. Lofton if I could manage to visit my dying father, she told me, "Just go, right now, it's your father," even though technically I wasn't supposed to travel for six more weeks.

"It feels like a spirit trip," I told Ken. "Like it's going to be okay." I turned up the heat and aimed it at my torso.

"Did I tell you about the dream I had last night?" he asked.

"What dream?"

"Well, I was just waking up, and I heard your dad's voice. He said, 'You know why I'm still here?'"

I could hear my dad's voice speaking those exact words. "Yeah, and what did you say?"

"I said, 'No, why are you still here?' And he said, 'I'm waiting for Caryn.'"

It would be amazing if Ken's dream were true. My father had never seemingly waited for me for anything. My father, who barely kept in touch, and whenever I called, would talk to me for just five minutes or so, and then say, "Gotta go. Give Ken my best." My father who, from my teenage years onward, had soundly and repeatedly rejected me in one vivid Technicolor scene after another.

But then I reminded myself that our fights and misunderstandings, our huge misinterpretations of each other's gestures and words, layers of old storylines dictating the current ones, all were part and parcel of our personalities. Maybe underneath it all there was something else, like the glimpse of him I had last September, when he asked if I recognized him. Maybe he sensed we weren't merely two totally different people living totally different lives.

By the time the plane touched down, it was nearly midnight, but I scrambled up the ramp to a quiet place where I could call the house. We debated whether to drive straight there, although we probably wouldn't arrive until 2 a.m., or wait until the morning.

My brother-in-law, Rick, who had recently left the military and planned to run the family business after Dad's death, answered. Yes, he was still alive. No, it didn't look like he'd be around long, and my brother Barry and his family had just visited. Rick consulted with my stepmother, who said we might as well just come in the morning.

I nervously explained all this to Ken, who was completely calm, "Don't worry, Caryn, he'll wait for you. He said he would."

"Why did he come to your dream and not mine?"

"Probably the channels were all busy in yours," Ken answered, and we claimed our luggage, and then our rental car, miraculously pre-heated for us in the zero-degree air. By the time we arrived at the three-star hotel I had snagged for a mere $40 and tried out the bed, I was half asleep. But I dozed only in jolts and snatches the whole night, waking suddenly to wonder if it were time to get up yet, while my exhausted body wished it could slap my noisy head out of the way for a good long rest.

The drive east, beginning at dawn, took over three hours thanks to tight traffic, narrow roads up and down mountains, and surprise appearances of little towns with long strips of fast food restaurants that necessitated many stoplights. We finally pulled onto my dad's street about 10 a.m.

I had tried to prepare myself to face a man who wouldn't look much like my father anymore, someone who would probably be completely bald now, free of the goatee he had worn for years, and very thin. What I found was my father. He looked more like himself than ever with thick hair and a full beard that covered much of his much-thinner face. A blanket hid most of his now child-sized body. He wore a white, pearl-button cowboy shirt with embroidered eagles on both sides. My stepmother ushered us into the former den, now inhabited by this hospital bed and a few chairs, plus a small table with medications and supplies. After she left us with him, I felt shy for a moment, not knowing how to begin or what to say, but Ken was right at home.

"Hey, Mel, thanks so much for waiting for us," he said, loudly and enthusiastically.

"Yeah, thanks for waiting for us," I added. "It was really good of you," I added a little more quietly.

"You're looking very comfortable," Ken said, "and that's a great shirt. Everyone's here now, and you can rest."

"We really love you, and we're all here for you."

"Yeah, we're all here for you now. You saw Barry yesterday, and all the kids have been around lately. And you've fought so hard for so long. You can rest now." I listened to Ken saying this, knowing I needed to say it, too.

"You can just relax and go, go in peace," I said. I looked at his open mouth, the bottom teeth that needed some serious orthodontic work, the smooth forehead, the huge eyes closed under long lashes; and listened to the slow, shallow breaths and the space in between. "You can go now. You've been very brave, and it's okay. We're all here for you."

"Yeah, we're all here for you."

We continued on like this for a few more minutes, then returned to the living room, right outside the den with its French doors open wide. Through them we could see my father's head and chest on the bed, the hospice nurse bending near to check him. My stepmother and stepsister explained that he had been slowing down for the last day. "He almost left yesterday," said Mary, my younger step-sister, who was still the same size and shape she was at 18, even though it was now three kids and many years later.

"And then a few days before that," added her mother.

"Yeah, he keeps tricking us," Mary said. "We kept wondering what he was waiting for, and then Barry got here yesterday, and so we figured he must still be hanging around to see you."

I knew he couldn't see me, but I also figured that, somehow or other— through sound or some other kind of knowing—he sensed me there. Had he really been waiting for me all this time? A minute later, I knew it had to be true, because my stepmother leapt up and rushed to my father's side, all of us following. She had been watching his chest, which no longer rose and no longer fell. All at once, I knew my father had waited for me even if he couldn't open his eyes or say a word.

I volunteered Ken to pick up my other stepsister, Wendy, while Mary, who had burst into tears, paced back and forth in the foyer just beyond the living room, making frantic phone calls. The area near my father's bed emptied as people went to make calls or to fetch others. Finally, just my stepmother, the hospice nurse, and I were left in the room.

My stepmother held my father's hand and pressed his forehead. Not wanting to impose, I put my palm over his knee, which, surprisingly, still had a pulse. The hospice nurse leaned up from listening to his heart. "He's taking about two breaths a minute. It won't be long now."

"Mel, you can go now. You've been so strong, and you've waited for everyone. Now you can go fly with the eagles. That's why I put that shirt on you. You've taken such good care of us, and now you can go."

Although my stepmother and I had never really gotten along, I tried to give her as much space as I could. I joined in, "It's okay, Dad, you did great, and you can go in peace now. You're free, and we all love you, and even after you go, we'll carry you in our hearts."

"Still getting a pulse in that knee?" the nurse asked.

I was, but it was harder to feel. "Maybe, kind of, it feels funny though."

My stepmother asked if she could feel his pulse, too, so I moved to the other side of the bed and held his other knee, but there was no pulse because there no longer was a pulse. The death was quiet and gentle, his breath slowing down in triple slow motion until we couldn't even say when it stopped. I never imagined death would be this ordinary, this simple. I never imagined my father would wait for me and let me share in this moment. I knew, despite all the pain that followed, that the way he died was a gift to me, even if his death was the opposite.

He had waited for me, maybe for the first and most important time in our life together.

After that came a marathon of phone calls, hugging my stepsisters and crying, more phone calls. Ken picked up various relatives around town. Barry, my brother from New Jersey, his wife Tammy, and their two kids poured into the house. Wendy's sons, especially one my father had been more a father to than a grandfather, showed up. Most people took a few minutes alone with him, emerging sobbing or stone-faced before heading to the kitchen for coffee. After a few hours, the rabbi, a Colombian man with whom my dad had become fast friends, arrived. He gathered us in the small den around my father's body, and covered him up in the middle of us. He also made sure the window was open.

"You," the rabbi said to me, "you just flew in?"

"Yes, but my arms are awfully tired," I answered, although it was a tired joke.

"Your father's daughter, that's what you are," the rabbi said, and we all laughed.

"This body," he told us, "is no longer your dad and husband and Mel. He's gone." We all nodded, and it seemed remarkably true to me that he was completely gone, vanished without a trace.

"But we keep the window open, and why do we do that? We keep it open just a crack so the spirit can get out."

We all nodded again in the room still warm despite the January air.

Cream Puffs

My father loved cream puffs, so when the caterer called back I ordered them along with a light meal for whoever showed up at the house after the funeral and burial services. I loved cream puffs too.

Meanwhile, the organizing of grief consumed us. The rabbi had told us that between the time Dad died and the burial, we were not yet official mourners but in some kind of limbo, and we should do whatever got us through. Considering that the "whatever got us throughness" of our family was food, my brother's family, Ken and I headed out for lunch. It was nearly 4 p.m., and we were all starving, so we descended upon a huge salad bar at some chain sit-down restaurant.

"Unbelievable," Barry said.

"Incredible," I answered. We talked over the details of what we had just lived through, while my nephew mixed chocolate pudding with peaches, much to his parents' dismay.

"Here, eat this shrimp, it's too much," I said to my sister-in-law.

"Nah, I'm full. I just can't."

"Oh, please."

"Let it go," Ken told me. "We just have too much food."

The next morning, at another chain restaurant sporting fake antiques on the wall, we had too much food again over breakfast with my sister, Lauren, who had flown in from Florida the night before. My youngest sister, Jennifer, couldn't go to the funeral because she had another attack of pancreatitis, the irony of which wasn't lost on me the day my father died of pancreatic cancer. We finished too quickly and had hours to wait until the funeral, hours we should have spent sleeping considering that Lauren and I had stayed awake in the dark motel room talking about every detail of Dad's death, each person's reactions, our own, until late into the night, our conversation punctuated only by Ken saying, "Please go to sleep already, you two!"

After breakfast, we spied a newspaper machine and pooled all our change to buy some copies. I went outside the restaurant in the falling snow and returned with three papers and just a little guilt. Seated next to giant muffins that stared at us constantly, we each took a paper and hunted down the obituary. Lauren's last name was spelled wrong. My last name was listed as Ken's last name. Still, there was something about seeing it in print that made the death more real. We each took the obituary section of our respective papers and left the rest for future breakfast-eaters to enjoy.

Because we had a lot of time on our hands, we started driving—Ken and I in the lead, and Lauren following in her car. We didn't have any idea where to go, so we circled around town, watching the houses in the snow pass by like dim lights, spotting gas stations, and, most importantly, finding the funeral home. Then we started heading toward the edge of town that melded with the mountain to the north, and before we knew it, we were climbing that mountain, finding tier after tier of reservoir, linked together by canals and waterfalls.

The snow grew thicker, the woods grew thinner, the climb more vertical than horizontal. The sky was swallowed up by the trees and snow in front of us as we climbed into the Allegheny Mountains. Soon, we were on top of the forest-covered mountain, the sky opening back up, and the trees suddenly smaller, wind-swept. The three of us got out of our cars, hats on and hands in pockets, looked around to see more snow and forest. We nodded at each other, got back into the car, and headed down.

We entered the funeral home from the back, surrendered our coats, and headed into the room where the beautiful, but simple, wooden coffin lay. All the walls here were quietly tan with oak trim gleaming in the soft lamp light. I stood with Ken, waiting to say something to the coffin that held my father's lifeless body, while Barry's wife, Tammy, held tight to my stepsister Wendy, saying, "It's God's plan, and all of this is what God would have wanted." I remembered how grateful I was months before when Tammy told me she had had her Baptist church pray for me.

The service was short and mostly in Hebrew, except for a eulogy from the rabbi who recalled meeting my dad for the first time and thinking that he was a Hassidic Jew come to challenge him. Actually, Dad was as non-practicing a Jew as one could be. Then the rabbi, who had previously asked me to do this, called me up to say a few comments.

I walked to the front and looked out. My step family was in the first row, and in the second row, my siblings. I told the story of my father asking me, last September, if I recognized him, and how this moment was a great gift to me, a moment to glance into my dad's soul. I thanked my step family and mumbled something about how we had to carry my dad in our hearts now, although I still heard his voice in my head.

When I was done, my siblings and step-siblings leapt up and bundled me in hugs. I shook as I made my way back to my seat.

The cold at the burial site was overwhelmingly biting as we stepped out into the ice and snow to climb a very steep little hill toward the grave. The clumps of people from dad's work, the synagogue, and the family soon tightened around the grave, situated on a slope beside a tall, mature pine tree. Ken, Barry, and the other pall bearers carried the coffin and placed it over the opening in the ground, then it was lowered down. Hebrew words sprung from the rabbi and others. When it was time, the coffin was released down, and the rabbi told us to grab shovels or even handfuls of dirt and start pouring them on the grave. Some people leaned on the arms of others, and some cried hysterically. I stared soberly at the hole in the ground.

Meanwhile, I noticed Ken at the foot of the grave, shoveling furiously, and my brother, at the very top of the grave, shoveling steadily. Because the land tilted so much in this spot, my brother seemed on a higher plane than me, though he was just six feet away. Snow continued to fall, a strange sheet of movement around us as we stood there, very still. My sister, watching my brother for a few moments, soon collapsed into tears, and I saw her, about 10 feet from me, making gestures that told me she was yelling and crying while a tall man in a leather jacket tried to soothe her. Later I would find out that she had been screaming at my dad, "Where were you on our birthdays? Why didn't you treat us better?" She also cursed him out in particularly colorful language. I learned later that as Barry shoveled and Lauren yelled, my brother's wife calmly pointed out, "Barry, you missed a spot."

Back at the house, we were expected to wash our hands with water, as per the Jewish burial ritual, before entering. A small ceramic bird bath near the door beckoned as each of us bent over and dipped our hands into the cold. My hands were both numbed and pained by the immersion, which felt right.

Inside, we sat or stood in a circle in the living room, prayer books in our hands. The rabbi tried to explain responsive reading, how he would read a section, and we would read the next, but with so few Jews in the room, some people got confused and simply read a repetition of what he'd just read. "No, no, no, let's start again. I read this part, and then you read the next part." Everyone got it the second time around.

When it was time for the Kaddish, the Hebrew prayer for mourning (really just a long list of prayers repeating "God is great" over and over), the rabbi placed books into my hands, my sister's and Barry's. As the only Jews in the room who were over Bat/Bar Mitzvah age, only we were allowed to say this prayer. We went slowly, and although I was afraid I wouldn't pronounce everything right, it didn't really matter as I eased into the familiar rhythm, my sister's and brother's voices walking through all the "yis-ga-dals" with me, all learning to travel here together.

Then there was food—salmon cakes, bagels, chocolates, tomatoes, cheesecakes. I loaded my plate and got a glass of water, handed to me in the kitchen by a man I didn't know who was doing everything he could to help the mourners. I balanced it all as I headed toward the couch, sat down, and tried to eat. But everything seemed too complex and difficult to take in, and in the end, all I could actually eat was the cream puff, one of the best damn cream puffs I've ever tasted.

Snow Storm

Back home in Kansas a few days later, we opened the door a little before 7 p.m. to greet a few dozen people balancing the food they'd brought and trying to climb out of their winter coats. They had come to say Kaddish with me at sunset. Usually, in our community, people showed up for two consecutive nights of Kaddish, although the official period of mourning, or "sitting Shiva," lasted a week, and actually extended through the whole first year plus all anniversaries of the death and birth of the deceased.

The first night we'd tried to do this, a snow storm kept the members of our congregation stuck in town and our family in the country, but now, though the roads were still wet and slick, people filled our kitchen table and counter with casseroles, desserts, and breads, the holy trinity of comfort foods for the living. I remembered that the last time so many of these people made their way to our place was six years ago for Forest's bris (circumcision), when I had hidden myself, wisely I might add, in the back bedroom and cried with some of my friends.

Now we held forth in a small circle in the living room, passing out small black booklets. The rabbi welcomed everyone, my kids sitting in unusual quiet on the couch. I thanked everyone for coming while telling a little about my father, how he and I were born on the same date, but hardly ever seemed to get along, and how his death—his waiting for me and dying with me present—was a kind of miracle between us. Saying the prayers was like stepping back into worn, old clothing that I had forgotten I even had. Afterwards, Artie, one of the men my father's age, came up to me and put his arm around me. "I had that kind of relationship with my father too," he said.

"How is it for you now?" I asked.

"Better," he said, as we walked arm-in-arm to the noodle kugel.

A few mornings later, something odd happened. Sometime around 6 a.m., the room gray with half-light, at that hour when night meets day, I was awakened by the chords of "Somewhere My Love."

I sat up abruptly in the dim light. Across from me, on a book shelf against the wall, sat my music box, a painted ceramic piano, broken and pieced back together decades ago. My mother had painted it at a ceramic studio in 1972 as a gift for me. The music mechanism had been broken for years, and the ceramic piano, the only object to survive my childhood, stood silently on my shelf, occasionally getting dusted, more often just overlooked.

Yet today the music box played the chorus of the song, not just once or twice, but many times. The only other sound was the faint rumbling of our soon-to-be-broken-beyond-repair used washing machine, doing its break-dance spin cycle on the other side of the wall to which the book shelf was bolted.

You could say the music box was jolted back into service by the shaking wall. You could say it must have been wound to its fullest, and that was why it played its song repeatedly. That it was all a matter of coincidence.

You could also say that the washer's spin cycle had shaken that wall every day for years, and yet the music box didn't play until now, and that it was no coincidence that the little ceramic piano was the one object in the room that dated back to the time when I lived in the same house with my father and mother, long before divorce ripped up our family. It was the perfectly logical object for my father to use.

Ken, when I told him later, was dubious. Having seen a ghost many years before when he was in his twenties, he tended to believe that the dead were less ambiguous in their communication; that they could dazzle us with a clear presence if they chose. Other people I told were absolutely convinced it was my father, come back to let me know he was close by, and that all the signs pointed clearly and absolutely to this fact.

Just to hedge my bets, from my seat in my bed, the blankets still gathered around me in the gray light brightening in the extraordinarily peaceful room, I spoke to the chimes of the music box. "Dad, if that's you, thanks so much for coming. And please do whatever you can to look after the kids and Ken and me. Please take care of us. Protect us."

Then I lay down again, as the Dr. Zhivago theme song cycled around to its slow ending, and fell deeply asleep, remembering that scene in the movie, even though it had probably been 30 years since I saw it, when Dr. Zhivago and Laura rode in a covered sled through miles of snow, the light ringing around them like a chorus of bells.

Key West

About ten days after Dad died, I found myself obsessing about Key West, a place I had never been. I opened the atlas to Florida every day, repeatedly, and stared at the Keys, the thin string of islands 150 miles long, suspended between the Atlantic ocean and the Gulf of Mexico. I picked up the laptop and spent hours searching for deals, guest houses, maybe campgrounds (once I saw the price of lodging on the Keys), swimming with dolphin excursions, detailed maps.

I learned about Key Largo, Marathon, the lower Keys, the middle Keys, and, 67 miles southwest of Key West, the Dry Tortugas, which one website claimed were mosquito-free. I read about Hemingway, Jimmy Buffet, and the best recipe for Key Lime pie. While out with my three kids, I steered them to bookstores (which didn't take much persuasion) so I could open piles of guidebooks about Florida, especially the ones covering Miami and the Keys. All I needed was a cheap flight from Kansas City to Miami, then a car to rent for the long drive. One travel day of sitting in small spaces, being flung through the universe at high speeds, waiting in many lines, and then speeding above the water on 42 bridges, some as long as 17 miles, and I could be there with Ken, staring at the end of the world.

Occasionally, I would look up and see the bleak light, the overcast sky, the grass and trees drained of all color as they are in January, especially during this, a drought year. My toes were perpetually cold, I wore a scarf all the time, even with my pajamas, and there weren't enough blankets each night. So I would step outside in the morning, bracing myself to turn the key in the ignition before picking up the ice scraper and applying it to the front windshield, all the time thinking of Key West. Turtles. Birds migrating. Palm trees. Snorkeling. Glass-bottom boats. Breakfast served by the pool, and the pool surrounded by a tropical garden. Conch fritters at roadside stands.

Knowing why I was obsessed with Key West didn't stop me from being obsessed. I was running away from grief, throwing myself into hours on the computer answering emails and writing reports for work, and then savoring the moments I could research the Keys. It was either this, or what I really wanted to do: climb back into bed, pull up the covers, and dream perpetually. Speak to no one. Play dead.

The whole time I'd been going through cancer, six months of chemotherapy, one surgery after another, I felt like one of those kid's toys from the 1980s, the Weebles who wobble but don't fall down. I would curl up in bed for an afternoon of deep depression, or walk shakily from the car to my favorite coffee shop to order my tea. It was hard, but there were always things to look forward to. The recovery from surgery. The doctor's visit deeming me upright and working well. The last week of each chemo cycle, when I would feel a little lighter and more like myself, and then the end of chemo itself. These were lights on the horizon to walk toward, even when I was encased in deep tangles of bramble and branch, the trees too thick for me to see the open sky very clearly. There was home ahead, a short or long distance, and all I needed to do was sleep through, or read through, or work through the hours ahead. It was simply one foot in front of the other while willing the wheels of time to turn a little faster.

But the territory of grief was very different. At first glance, it looked the same—big open spaces, thick forests, greeting cards from people I didn't realize cared about me, long drought-stricken stretches of wasteland, high phone rates (and no real discounts), sudden heat that lasted for hours, cold I couldn't get away from, and blacktop so extensive I thought I was in a deserted stadium parking lot. But once I started fumbling around in this new place, I realized it wasn't any place I'd ever known before.

People would ask me how I was doing. "Okay," I said often, but then added the answer they wanted: "Yes, it's been too much lately, but I'm doing fine considering." I wasn't fine or okay. I would order food in a restaurant, and when it arrived, it seemed all wrong, and I found I could only eat a taste of the giant cinnamon roll in front of me. I would lie down and get up. I would read the sympathy cards with excitement and then get depressed. I would receive an email stating that a meeting date was changed, and I would feel devastated. I would answer the phone excitedly and start talking to a friend only to find, a few minutes later, that I wanted to hang up and go to sleep. I would plan menus, go shopping, put the groceries away, and then find I had no will to actually cook anything.

Food rotted in the refrigerator. Calls went unanswered. Much of the house piled up with papers and clothing, all totally beyond my control. Bills went unpaid. Cats slept beside me, ignored. Little routines at home or at work became great challenges of spirit for me.

With my kids, I felt myself becoming a kind of hybrid Stepford mother. I answered their questions, drove them to their lessons, asked them about school and homework and friends, bought them frozen pizzas and soy yogurt like always. When they yelled in the car, I yelled back, "Shut up! I'm going to have an accident or something if you keep fighting" just like I always did, then regretted telling them to shut up, just as I always did. But I knew, and I suppose they knew too, that I wasn't really there.

When I called my mother, I tried to think of questions to ask her, relatives to check up on, but my memory failed me. With Judy, I simply told her I was too tired to meet, glad I could be honest even if I didn't know what being honest was at the moment.

To add to the confusion, I experienced none of the bargaining or denial I'd expected. I couldn't say whether I actually missed Dad or at least the possibility of how he could have been. It felt more like something huge, like the weight of all my bones, was gone forever. Something ripped out from the center of my life. The loss was so devastating I didn't see how I would ever get over it, or even reach the point where I could get up off the ground. Or stop crying sometimes, when driving alone. Or cry to the bottom of all this.

In the wake of such a loss, what other people talked about or did seemed utterly bizarre and frivolous. "Why are people sending me fucking jokes over the fucking email?" I asked Ken. Why was I ordering a café au lait with whipped cream just like I always did? Why was junk mail coming to the house along with phone calls about contributing to the highway patrol? Why was I watching so many bad movies, my sole criteria that they must be comedies, and thinking those bad movies were actually great? Where was my taste? Where was my sense of outrage? Where was my sense of humor? Where was I?

Lacking direction, I pretended to be just like the self I had been before, but really I didn't have any idea of where I was, where to go, or how to get there. Since I was so lost, it somehow made sense that the only place to be was simply at the end of the world, in Key West, where the earth stopped in the middle of vast and unfathomable ocean. A new kind of night, with its dark, windy, lingering warmth, wrapped around me.

Chapter Nine: Breastless

Woman Who Swims with Stingrays

Key West happened. I had a conference to attend in Miami, so Ken flew down, rented a car, picked me up from the lobby of the snazzy hotel where I had spent too much time riding the elevator during four days of meetings, and we headed south down lush boulevards lined with palm trees, then bare stretches of trailer homes and trashed out bowling alleys. It was a four-hour drive to the small guest house where we would spend three nights, a place that didn't even allow kids (I had never stayed in, let alone imagined, such a place before) nestled tight in Old Town.

There were so many islands along the way, and the sky was open and blue, the ocean flooded with turquoise light, the world open and happy. We were on our first trip ever more than an hour from home without the kids, thanks to friends, babysitters, and Ken's parents, not to mention a freezer full of frozen pizzas. We were taking my breasts, "the girls," as I was referring to them by this point, out for a final spin before the surgery set for Earth Day.

Island after island, big flashes of ocean followed by blurs of trees and dense pockets of forest (but no sightings of the famous miniature deer of the Keys, which Ken called "deeritos"), and then vast stretches of ocean, especially when we got to the 17-mile bridge that took us over an exhausting ocean. To my right, I saw an older, deserted bridge, now home to pelicans that hovered near its torn edges and squawked at the tourists zipping by on the main bridge. They were on their road to nowhere, but then again, so were we.

By the time we arrived, after getting lost for only fifteen minutes in the white-housed, tropical-gardened, utterly tasteful streets of Old Town, it was late afternoon. We were given the key to our room, small but habitable, with a tiny porch overlooking a cement pond where an iron fish spouted a steady stream of water back into water. We turned on the ceiling fan and the air conditioner, took off all our clothes, like we never could at home, and napped in the dim light of that pale turquoise room.

Later, I waded unsteadily on the shifting sand into the water, at the southernmost point of the United States, feeling the ocean swim and rock over my breasts, and reminded myself that this was the last time I would feel this sensation. When I showered or sat in the hot tub or stuffed my breasts into their bra, I was constantly aware of how little time I had left with this part of the body, this part of my sensual life.

But when we made love, I found myself filled with despair, each touch catalyzing a flood of sadness. Although the loss wasn't happening until April 22nd; I realized it had already started: my body seemed fully aware of the violence heading its way and yet, at the same time, like an innocent lamb, oblivious to the plans my busy mind and mouth had made for it. I slept each night, during this trip, and afterwards, holding my breasts. Even when I made a conscious choice to keep my hands elsewhere, I awoke with them back on my breasts, keeping them from going anywhere.

After a few days of island exploring, walking something like 13 miles, eating ample quantities of Cuban, Bahamian and other foods, and, one afternoon, accepting a ride with drunk locals driving a golf cart while laughing and swerving, we finally went snorkeling on our last night in Key West.

The boat was filled mostly with kids and their parents, the last stream of spring break students, and a few other adults, all headed out from the island. My study of Key West on maps didn't show all the other islands, small and smaller, seemingly floating on the ocean like scattered plastic bags. Some were empty, some full of high-rise hotels.

Finally, the boat stopped, and everyone geared up in snorkels, flippers, and goggles and prepared to climb down into the water. The coral reef here would be orange and bronze, according to the guide. But as we were descending into the water, I looked all around me and saw nothing but ocean, no solid ground. I panicked in just the same way I did years before, when I took an elevator to the bottom of a shaft to explore a massive cave in South Dakota, and a tour guide announced, "We're the equivalent of 40 stories underground." My anxiety attack was so acute that the guide had to take me back to the surface, and then return to lead the tour while I sat above ground, hyperventilating.

It didn't help matters that the tour guide proceeded to warn everyone to stay in one specific area because, if we strayed, we would be in "Stingray City."

"It's okay," Ken said as he bobbed in the water, reaching his hand out to me. But I couldn't stop shaking, my stomach trembling, my whole body made of fear at the moment. I dropped into the water, felt its chill, and panicked some more, grabbing hold of Ken's hand in a death grip. The motion of the water kept threatening to knock me over.

"I can't do it, we have to go back, it's too scary."

"It's okay. It's just the ocean, and we'll see some coral reefs."

The waves lifted and dropped us, threatening to overtake my head unless I kept myself upright until I, a good swimmer, was terrified of drowning. It took me a long time before I could calm down enough to put my face into the water, telling myself snorkeling was all about breathing and moving, breathing and moving.

Eventually, holding hands tightly, we swam a little, seeing the rust-colored coral, starfish, round breathing things, little quick fish darting by. Inhale, exhale, I told myself. Inhale some more. Carefully. Keep my head tilted upright enough to avoid inhaling water when a wave swept over. But of course I did, and immediately shot my head out of the water.

Breathe, breathe, breathe. I held Ken's hand tighter, and to his credit, he didn't once complain about the marks I was leaving on him, as strong as any marks I had left on his palms during childbirth. We went back under, and I was starting to relax, lifting my head every so often to make sure we didn't swim with the stingrays. It was okay, I was seeing fish, I was seeing coral, I was seeing a whole autumnal-colored picture of the underworld. It was beautiful: the shapes of small, wind-worn cities beneath us, complete with crowds of miniature fish swimming in and out of the brown and rust structures of old ruins or live plants

When I finally relaxed enough to let go of Ken's hand, a stingray zoomed by so close that it skimmed my torso.

I bolted upward, freaking out. Ken met me there. "It's okay. It won't hurt us." After a lot of reassurance and aiming ourselves back toward the boat, I dove back under. Breathe, breathe, breathe. Relax.

That's when I saw the barracuda. About a foot away from me. It was huge, almost the size of our ten-year-old.

I didn't know it was a barracuda, though. "Shark," my mind said. "Shark ready to attack."

The panic filled me like pins and needles. But soon, we were safely back on deck, heading fast toward an old shipwreck, where I would swim with more ease and actually get to the point where I could swim alone over the decaying wreckage of the past, my soon-to-be-departed breasts passing over old planks and blue fish, and a thousand miniature breathing stars clinging to the side of a rusted anchor.

That night, walking down decadent Duval Street, I found an angel. A transvestite angel, to be exact. She wore all-white angel attire, her head in a gleaming turban. I stopped before this angel, and reached into my purse to find a dollar to place in her porcelain bowl as I looked into the angel's eyes. She looked back at me, lifted her arms to the sky majestically, and then reached out and embraced me. I held the angel close to my heart. Then the angel released me, and I went home.

The Passover Miracle

About 20 people were milling about the living room on this brilliant early evening, ready to find their seats and start the Seder, enough wine finally here after someone went back into town, enough gefilte fish, eggs, salad, dessert, matzoh, charoset, and enough eggplant shepherd's pie, the main dish we'd eaten together for almost two decades. Some of the approximately 30 people we had invited over for Passover were still in the living room, puzzling over where best to sit at the L-shaped configuration of rented tables and assorted chairs. The seating arrangement worked well so long as no one exhaled.

As always, Judy and her husband Stan were there, along with my friend Reva, who specialized in the matzoh ball soup each year, and her family, and other friends older and younger, mostly Jewish or kind of Jewish or just so much a part of our Seder for so long that they were here. Courtney and Denise had been in the kitchen for hours helping me sweep and mop; Reva came early to put the massive pot of soup on the stove. Now it was time.

Just as everyone was putting a hand on the back of a chair or sitting down, the bird crashed.

Maybe the dog was chasing it, or maybe it just got confused, but it flew into the house, hit a window trying to get out, and landed in a plant. Courtney went over, squatted down, and tended to the bird. Her long, slender hands could build a pond (she had built one with me in our greenhouse recently), knit a dozen hats, milk a goat, or sort mail at the speed of light. If anyone could help this bird, she could. She rose slowly as I walked over to her.

"Is it dead?"

"Not yet," she said, showing me a tiny grayish, bluish thing, a titmouse, we would find out later from the bird book, "but it's dying now."

I watched its leg twitch, its small eyes darting in terror, its quiet torso. We felt sad, and soon kids were gathering around to see the dying bird. Natalie looked especially startled, her eyes filling as she watched in horror. Courtney held the bird quietly, then headed outside to find it a burial spot.

Maybe it was the wind, or the last dark light from the west hitting it, or just the bird coming to its senses, but suddenly, that almost-dead bird shot out of her hand and into the sky, off to the woods. I remembered how, last week, my friend Jolene had told me she had dreamed that I was to be liberated from my breasts, and it was a dream full of light and good humor.

"I guess it was just stunned," Courtney said.

"Ah, Hon," said Denise, "it was just the Passover miracle." She had grown her Mohawk out. Denise smiled and twirled a little in her bell-shaped wedding dress that she wore for these kinds of occasions. I loved when her dimples showed.

We took our seats, began the ancient ritual, the old-time celebration of liberation and freedom, the last Passover before my mastectomy, I told myself, liberation and freedom coming, but at such a cost. I lifted my cup of wine with the others, singing out the prayers, laughing at the occasional good blending of our voices that added up to far more than the sum of our parts.

Show Us Your Hooters

That's what the bumper sticker said on the truck right in front of me at the stoplight. It was two days before my breasts would be cut off, and here I was, confronted with a giant bumper sticker to remind me I lived in a world where women's breasts were the central focus of men. Other reminders abounded, such as the way women's clothes were constructed with perfectly-placed darts to highlight breasts. Breasts in bras. Breasts in bikinis. Breasts under sweaters. Breasts filling out T-shirts. Breasts under jackets and inside pullovers. Breasts peeking over the top of a shirt or hiding safely inside.

Lots of women, in the weeks before my surgery, asked me how I felt about losing my breasts.

"Sad."

One day, the sadness got so overwhelming that I wandered into a medical supply shop to look over the fake boobs. I was in a vulnerable mood. A man walked up to me, offering to help.

"I'm so freaked out right now that I'm trying to distract myself by holding a silicon breast," I thought. But what I really said was, "I'd like to see your mastectomy supplies."

He went to get a saleswoman for me. I heard her say, "I'm really busy now. Can't Debbie help her?" Then she swept past me, as if I wasn't there, and I waited several minutes for the other woman.

"Hello there. How may we help you today?" she said, her blond head tipping toward me with the smile she had just pasted on her face to make the sale.

"I'm having a mastectomy next week, and I'd like to see the prostheses you carry."

She led me to a private room, showed me the soft camisole they carried, the type with pockets to put the soft forms inside. She let me hold one, something made of fluff and tissue, the kind of thing I used to consider stuffing in my bra when I was teenager. Then she handed me the silicone breast, expensive enough to account for its flesh-like feel, its temperature cool as a regular breast, its weight just like something human and made of skin, but also somewhat like a play toy. I explained I would probably like one that drooped a little, that I didn't want to look too perky here. She showed me another model, again soft, heavy, cool, flesh-colored. I wondered if they carried these things in different shades of brown for women whose skin wasn't my color, or how I would feel wearing a differently-colored breast.

I took the brochures and thanked her.

Trying to feel normal, I sent out a lot of emails, asking for prayers, making jokes like suggesting that on Earth Day (or "Caryn-gets-liberated-from-her-breasts Day") all the women I knew should dance topless on tables in coffeehouses.

"I'm gonna be drinking a lot of coffee on Earth Day," one man wrote back.

Women wrote that they would at least dance topless at home, and one retired psychiatrist I knew, a quiet, conservative, no-nonsense guy, wrote that he would dance topless on a table, if need be. I collected the emails, printed them out, made a pile of wishes and prayers to take with me to the hospital, words to fortify me against the oncoming loss.

Meanwhile, every time I hugged another woman, I was more aware than ever before of her breasts against my breasts, the space between us filled in a way that it would not be later. Women with big breasts would tell me they had extra I could have transplanted onto me, and we would laugh. Women with naturally flat chests would tell me that now I'd know how they felt.

After a while, I found myself watching small-breasted, flat-chested women with far more interest than ever before—how their shirts hung on them, how they still looked like women, graceful and nurturing and sexy and feminine. I started watching them carefully to see how beautiful they were, and they always were.

"Breasts are huge for me," a man said to Ken. "Isn't this hard for you?"

Ken looked at the guy like he was from another planet. "It's nothing," he told the man, "compared to Caryn keeping her life."

The ground kept shifting. I told myself, using every phrase I could think of, to tell myself what was going to happen: double mastectomy, breasts lopped off, bilateral mastectomy, breasts cut off, deboobing, mammatus interruptus, breast removal, titty termination, hooter annihilation, boob-away, boobectomy. Even one Daniel made up: de-racking. The landscape of my body was to change, drastically.

Yet I realized that I was giving up my breasts willingly. A willing sacrifice. A letting go in the name of life. A release from the body, for the body.

That night, after I finished cleaning the last of the dishes, Forest came into the kitchen. He should have been sleeping, but instead, he was still in his T-shirt, a Sponge Bob version stained with spaghetti sauce, and sweat pants. His eyes looked at me intently and shyly at the same time.

"Hey, Mom," Forest said, in the typical way he began his every sentence addressed to me, coming at a fast clip. "Are you done with this cancer?" Now I saw that he had also spilled jelly on the front of his shirt, and his face had something tomato-y on it.

"Yeah, I think so, I mean, I still have the surgery ahead." I pointed to my breasts to remind him, and then put some of the wine glasses up on the highest shelf.

"Oh, what surgery?"

"The one to remove my breasts. You remember that."

"Will they grow back?" he asked earnestly. His blue eyes looked as if he had never seen anything but goodness his whole life, which might have been true. He must have thought of breasts as hair or fingernails.

"No, but I'll get some little fake breasts to wear inside my bra so that I'll still look the same."

He nodded. "You sure they won't grow back?" he asked, a little puzzled.

"Yeah, I'm sure, and close the refrigerator, okay?"

He shut the door and came over to hug me. "Um, Mom," he said, "it's too bad that they won't grow back."

Burying the Breasts

It was an unusual spring night because it was windless, something uncommon for Kansas in April. But it was dark and sweet, the scent of just-opening lilies-of-the-valley and lilac lacing the air on this eve of my mastectomy.

Once we got the kids in bed, the house finally quiet enough to slip away without anyone noticing, we stepped outside our bedroom door onto the deck, Ken with a shovel and me with several pages of paper and a candle. The candle was shaped like a flower, petals of pink wax tinged with rosy edges, and I lit it quickly. It was strange to watch the flame remain lit, not even faltering, as Ken and I walked into the dark yard and up the hill behind our house. I didn't think I'd ever successfully light a candle outdoors in Kansas because of the constant movement of the air.

We climbed the hills carrying our wares. Already, my throat was a little dry, and I knew I wouldn't be allowed even water between now and sometime after the surgery. We walked up a path we had made simply by walking it, over dead tree branches, leaf-covered ground, between cedar trees and under Osage Orange trees, until we were most of the way up the hill. We arrived in a small clearing, my thighs sore.

"Here," I told Ken. I placed the candle at the base of a tall cedar tree and unfolded the pages. I read about the gratitude I had for my bones, blood, organs, and the spaces in between, which together gave me life breath by breath, that carried me through growth and healing, that made my life possible and holy in this holy body.

I thanked my breasts for protecting my heart, bringing me pleasure, feeding my children, filling out my clothes, balancing my hips, adding roundness to me, softening my edges. I read my intentions for this surgery: my wish for enough strength, courage, faith, and love to grow in spirit through all aspects of the surgery, my wish to live, my desire to heal from all the effects, my trust that all the people involved would do well, and my hope to open my heart after having gone through this.

I asked for guidance and healing, a way through, alertness and quick recovery, to go wherever I needed to go during these surgeries and to come back completely.

I looked up at Ken and could see tears on his face in the dappled light from the clouds above, the candle below, as he stepped on the shovel and pushed it into the ground. Once the earth was open, I placed all the pages I had read, carefully folded, in the space between the dirt, and we buried those words. I blew out the candle and left it at the base of the tree as a gift.

When we got home, Jerry called. "I'll be there," he said of the surgery.

"But don't you have to work?"

"There's no way I can work with this happening," he answered, more quickly than he usually spoke. I thanked my stars for this amazing friend and for the usual surgery team friends, who would stop their lives to help us through the next day. As I continued to talk with him, I felt the circle of quiet encompass me, Jerry's way of being present and available in this world.

The next morning we went to the hospital. I don't remember much, though. I vaguely remember only the prep room, where Judy came in and smiled, Laurie gave me a kiss, Jerry held my hand, and Ken watched over all of us while the nurse inserted the IV. Dr. Jew came in to say hello and to direct Ursula toward a pair of scrubs she could wear.

I don't remember being wheeled to the surgery room. I don't remember coming out of surgery, although I heard I threw up a little. I don't remember the room where they put me. I don't remember seeing Ken or Jerry or Laurie or Judy or Ursula. I don't remember talking with my mother on the phone. I don't remember Dr. Jew coming in to tell me everything looked great. I don't remember calling room service to order my dinner, or what I had for breakfast the next day.

After those earlier surgeries, I was vividly grateful to have returned from wherever my soul had wandered during surgery. I can picture myself signing the papers to leave the hospital after the hysterectomy, thrilled to release myself into the cold. There were balloons and flowers after the lumpectomy. After both of those surgeries, I was happy and relieved in the wheelchair as I was being escorted out of the hospital.

But years after this double mastectomy, I still cry as I write, as I revise, as I reread my own words, surprised at this lapse, stunned at what I've forgotten.

The Unbearable Lightness of Lilac

We arrived home to find the house still fairly messy. For some reason, the friend we'd hired to clean while we were at the hospital never came. Luckily, we also found a box waiting for us with some flowers in it, a wide bouquet of tulips from my sister Jennifer. And there was a second box with an assortment of lilies and roses and whatnot from my mom.

I lifted the flowers out of their plastic and placed them in their vases.

Then I looked at the house. How could I be in this place with dirty counters and floors, with papers and clothing and shoes flung all over, when I had just lost my breasts? How could I be in any place that wasn't orderly and filled with flowers?

"Go take a nap, please," said Ken. "I'll take care of it."

"I can't believe she didn't come to clean," I said, repeatedly.

"Just take a nap. It'll be okay."

"I can't. I have to clean."

"No, you shouldn't be bending and lifting. You just had surgery yesterday. Just go to the bedroom and try to rest."

I did try, you have to give me that. I went to the bedroom and opened the door. The floor was a mess, the bed was unmade, an old newspaper lounged on the floor, there was a glass plate with crumbs on the book shelf. I couldn't stand being in that room, I couldn't sit in it, I couldn't sleep there.

So I went back to the kitchen and then to the greenhouse, looking for the big orange clippers. I knew exactly what I had to do.

"What are you doing?" Ken asked, exasperated.

"I'm going for lilac."

"You just had surgery! I'll get you the lilac." I could see the tiredness in his eyes, how he just wanted to lift back up the newspaper he was holding, but I was relentless.

"Why aren't you cleaning?"

"I'm tired, I'll take care of it."

"No, I'll take care of it," I said, switching direction and heading toward the sink to wash dishes. "I'll do it like I always do it, like I always have to do it!"

"And what do you think I've been doing for the last year while you've been going through this? How dare you accuse me of not doing enough?"

I knew he was right, but I was too far gone to stop. "I didn't mean you."

"Yes you did, and you think it's my fault that the house isn't clean? Where have I been, Caryn? I've been with you at the hospital, I've been there for two days, and in between, Caryn, I've been calling in to work and taking care of the kids and making sure you're okay." When he used my name that much, I know I was in trouble, yet I still couldn't turn back.

"I know it's not you," I said, but I started crumbling fast, and knowing what a mess both the house and I were, I couldn't stand to have anyone see me. "Just leave me alone, just let me get some flowers!"

"Don't you dare go out that door!"

I went out the door, slamming it behind me, and walked purposefully toward my in-laws' house where giant bushes of dark purple lilac resided.

No matter that I was crying, shaking a little, maybe because of the effects of being put under and cut into, and maybe just out of shame and exhaustion. Still, I was on my own two legs, walking fast down the dirt road over the slight slope with Ken trailing behind me now, in the car, calling through the windows, "Get in the car, just get in the car already!"

I ignored him, cradling the large orange-handled clippers against my broken body, the big wind all over the place, sweeping through me. I walked quickly and upright despite whatever had been taken from me, despite the way my body was cut open again, this time parts slashed off, dissected and tested in great detail, my breasts a pile of blood and flesh in some lab where they would be disposed of, probably already inside some medical trash can.

I was heading toward blossoms, and nothing could stop me.

When I reached my mother-in-law's old-fashioned dark purple lilac, I reached up again, against the tightness of gauze and paper tape, against the odd sensation of my blank chest, against the soreness of my arms intent on taking back their old strength.

I cut and cut and cut, gathering against my chest the dark purple, the dark scent so alive with everything: death and birth, loss and blossom, breaking and falling. My arms filled with the explosion of lilac so dark and full, and then I moved to the white lilac bush and filled my arms even more, the wind pouring against me and through me.

When I had gathered enough lilac to cover me from my belly to the top of my head, I stopped and looked sideways toward the car. Ken was waiting quietly. He leaned over and opened the passenger door, and I got in, holding the lilac tight, still clutching the big clippers. He didn't say anything, his eyes caught between fury, exhaustion, sorrow, and tenderness. I looked away, burying my face into the blossoms.

Once home, I filled half a dozen vases with lilac, placing some in my bedroom, some in the living room, some on the kitchen table and counter. Ken went to do the dishes. In a few hours the kids would be home, but for now, with the flowers lifting this weighed-down house and heavy-handed body just enough, I could lie down. I could go to sleep.

My Beautiful Blood

When I woke, the three kids were bursting through the front door with backpacks and little arguments between them. In a flash, they were standing next to my bed.

"Do you feel okay?" Natalie asked. She was wearing a black T-shirt that had a Habitat for Humanity logo on it, and her long hair was wide and curly with humidity.

"Sure, I'm fine," I said, lifting the blanket to show them that underneath my T-shirt there were a lot of bandages over a flat chest.

"Now you look like me," Natalie said. The boys looked away shyly. My breasts had been a private thing they hadn't seen much of since their nursing days. Now my chest had changed, gone public to an extent, like a man or a girl before puberty.

Strangely enough, after some burritos and jokes with the kids about their day at school, I started to feel happy. I was done! I had gone through all the surgeries, the chemo, the losses. It was over.

But I did still have tubes hanging from me, big plastic suckers draining my blood, which I was supposed to squeeze into a plastic cup every hour or so, and then write down the amounts to call in to the surgeon's office.

"It's so beautiful," Forest said when he saw the tubes hanging out the bottom of the T-shirt. "Mom, you have such beautiful blood."

A day later, I walked to the deck. It was misting, but still warm. "There," I told Ken, pointing to a blank part of the lawn. "Couldn't I have it there?"

"Sure," he said. "Just go rest, okay?"

I did, and a few hours later when I went outside, there was a rectangle of dirt with lots of good top soil shoveled onto it. Ken was putting down a black mesh gardening sheet, the type you just cut holes into where you want to plant your flowers, and then there would be minimal weeding.

When he was done, he headed off to town to pick up the kids, and I walked outside to the site. It was perfect. I got out a book on the ideal cutting garden, a garden full of flowers to cut and put into vases. It was still early, and Ken had grocery shopping to do; he wouldn't be home for hours.

So I got into the car and drove to my favorite nursery, about 20 minutes away in the country. When I got there, I gingerly climbed out of the van, still a little sore, and selected a red wagon from their herd of little wagons. I was wearing a T-shirt with a sweater over it, but still, when I looked down, I was stunned by the absence, the new topography.

I looked up and saw an acquaintance, who didn't know much about what I had been up to, although I figured it was likely he had heard from mutual friends that I had cancer.

"Hi, how you doing?" he asked, his bald head gleaming in the sun, which had peeked out just out for a moment.

"Good," I said.

We both acted like my appearance was normal, but I felt awkward, embarrassed, like I didn't want to explain anything, but wasn't it all so obvious, anyway?

Back home, I carried the cardboard trays of plants and packets of seeds to the new plot. I started cutting holes in the black gardening cloak and then dug into the dirt to make room for each plant. I couldn't lean over as well as I had hoped because my arms and chest were too sore, so I lay down on the earth and stretched my body over each row as I planted. The sky had gone hazy again, and a light mist fell steadily. I kept adjusting my position, as I eased into the ground the cosmos seeds, snapdragons, larkspur, rudbeckia, zinnias, ageratum, reaching my arms, leaning my sore chest into the quiet and steady ground.

By the time I was done, I was covered in mud—my arms, my legs, my torso, especially my hands. Mud under the fingernails, mud in the hair. It was good.

That night, while watching a forgettable Italian film that moved so slowly I could barely follow it, I told Ken about seeing the acquaintance and how awkward I felt. He nodded and went to the car, then returned with some foam rubber and the electric carving knife he used at work to make wheelchair modifications for clients. I handed him a bra, a stretchy black one that I had previously worn all the time. "Used to wear" echoed in my mind.

I looked over the blue foam, kind of spongy, and then some lighter tan-colored foam, which I chose. I had to wear something between now and a month or so after surgery when I would be healed enough to get a pair of real fake boobs.

"How big do you want them?" he asked.

"How big do you want them?"

We both laughed as he carved me a pair of boobs, well-contoured and weighted just enough that they didn't keep trying to climb to my neck like the cotton inserts the hospital had given me. Okay, so they were more than a little perky, and occasionally, I needed to push them down when they gained a little too much ground toward my neck, but at least I had a counterbalance to my hips, something between my head and my stomach. I could put on my clothes and feel, at stray moments, like nothing all that drastic had changed.

The next day, I wore the stuff of cheap couches rounding out my chest, not far, mind you, just to my in-laws' for dinner. Their dining room felt like a comfortable pair of pajamas to me, a place I had inhabited for many years, eating large quantities of comfort food and having conversations that usually involved someone my father-in-law used to teach or what various far-flung family members were up to. Sitting around their table, just before we lifted forkfuls of the roast to our mouths, Forest piped up triumphantly, "Grandma and Grandpa, have you seen my mom's beautiful blood?"

Buying Boobs

It was spring, the trees in crazed blossom, and Judy, Natalie and I were on an expedition to Kansas City to buy boobs, my first real prosthesis. I wanted some help in picking out the right shape, right drape, something natural-looking, which translates into something kind of drooping and falling just right for a 43-year-old who had nursed three children.

The drive itself proved to be the first impediment. For some reason, I felt unduly nervous behind the wheel, which made me a little hesitant when it came to merging into big lanes on the big highway. That, in turn, made me drive more dangerously. As I pressed my foot to the floor to avoid hitting a black SUV, I could tell what Judy was thinking.

"I'm not driving so well," I said out loud.

"Yeah, I noticed," she said. "You just have to merge a little faster. Don't hesitate so much."

Finding the breast store wasn't nearly as difficult as finding a decent place for lunch. We ended up eating at a supermarket salad bar, sitting together with our assorted soggy fried chicken or salad. From there, it was off to get the goods, and in no time, we had squeezed ourselves into a very small room, about the size of a walk-in closet for the middle-class, where a lovely, older woman, elegant in her off-pink pantsuit and tasteful scarf, held up one silicon breast after another, like she was a model on "The Price is Right."

"I really want something that looks real," I told her.

"I know just what you need," she said, going to the shelves and pulling out what seemed like a big mama boob. If it were a hat, it would have covered the whole top of my head.

"But it's huge!"

"It's a size six, and I think that's really what you need to fill out the prosthesis bra," which I now had wrapped around me, a flattened version of what would look like a normal woman's chest once I slipped in the right forms.

"Well, it's the only size six anything I'll ever wear," I said.

It actually took very little time for me to figure out what size worked best, what weight, what shape, and within 20 minutes, I had selected the right bra and right set of breasts. Then followed 40 minutes of paperwork. Meanwhile, Judy and Natalie sat on a couch together, looking at the snapshots in Judy's wallet. Natalie was intrigued with Judy's uncle, how Judy looked as a girl, and especially Judy's two mothers. I was more focused on the getting of two matching breasts, which I had even hoped to wear home, like a new pair of shoes.

The paperwork proved to be the deal-breaker, however. My insurance didn't cover this lovely breast store.

"I'm so sorry you had to spend an hour with me, and you're not even getting a sale out of it," I told the breast-fitter as she wrote down the details of what bra and breast worked for me.

"It's fine," she said. "I do this all the time, and I'm happy to be here for you."

I apologized two or three more times, and then off we went again, back onto the treacherous highway, where I zoomed and merged, driving too fast or too slow all the way home.

A day later, I went to the local medical supplies shop and found a set of breasts that fit just as well as the ones in Kansas City. "Whipped silicon," I would tell my girlfriends at lunch, as I popped one out. Everyone passed it around, oohing and aahing at how real it felt.

In fact, I passed them around often, as if they were really cool party favors, whenever anyone asked me how I was. "I'm great. Want to see my new boob?" Usually people nodded, maybe out of curiosity, maybe out of politeness. After all, this was the Midwest. So my new boobs made the rounds in supermarket aisles, in the women's bathroom of the Jewish Community Center, among my exercise classmates when we met for coffee afterwards, and at assorted meetings. It was like having an amazingly cute rodent who did exotic tricks.

"I'm beginning to understand the allure of the female breast," my student Jeanne told me when, months later, she petted my breast on a porch in Colorado. My sister-in-law, who was fairly small-chested, immediately inserted them into her own bra and paraded around before her rolling-eyed teenage daughters. Several men put them on their heads and laughed. Of course my starter-breasts, the ones Ken carved for me, became a favorite dress-up item of my sons.

As for what lay beneath the movable feast, I found myself eager to flash anyone who was interested. There was something about showing the scars that made them less horrifying to me, that made them human, that made them accepted and ordinary, which was just what I needed. One afternoon, several women in my kitchen ended up in an impromptu scar-sharing party, ignited by Carol, who unzipped her pants to show us the long thick lines from her intestinal surgeries. Someone else showed her bikini scar from a Caesarian birth. I got to show off both the long blue line of the hysterectomy and the two long slashes across my chest. All our scars shone that afternoon, badges of some sort, traces of stories that had changed our lives.

Father's Day

I stood in front of the Father's Day card rack. Only three cards to buy—one for my father-in-law, step-father and husband. Nothing this year to take home, nag the kids to sign, and then send off to my own father.

When Father's Day arrived, it seemed like the phone had a red light on it, calling my attention to its inability to connect me to my dad for one of our usual holiday conversations: saying hello, telling what was happening that day, each of us saying our work was going fine and giving our family reports to family. I couldn't call my father, so I called my sister, Lauren, instead.

"It's weird, isn't it?" I asked.

"It's fucking weird," she said.

"I mean, if he's not alive anymore, where the hell is he?"

"Beats me, but it's just too fucking weird. Hey, did I tell you I had a dream about him? He was telling me to go ahead and speak to him even though he's dead. Usually, I just dream he's not dead yet, that it's the weekend of his dying, and we're all waiting around for him to go."

"I think he's with us all the time."

"Now that freaks me out," said Lauren, pausing, I could tell, to light a cigarette, probably somewhere on the deck of her Orlando house.

"Why?"

"Caryn, I don't want Dad around when I'm having sex!"

I had been dreaming about him too, but not that he was dying. In my dreams, he was firmly and completely dead although in one, I saw him as a newborn baby, just born. Mostly, though, I wondered awake about him: where did he go, and how did this happen?

I hung up the phone with Lauren, and walked outside into the field. It was a beautiful June day, but my father was dead. It was Father's Day but I didn't have a father anymore. The sky was filled with mackerel clouds, stretched horizon to horizon, the blue bleeding through.

"Dad," I said quietly, asking him yet again for protection and blessing. I looked around. Only the cat was listening. "Happy Father's Day."

Chapter Ten: Sky

Storm

Our first time together, almost 18 years ago now, was during a lightning and thunder storm that lasted all night. We were upstairs in Ken's tiny apartment on a futon on the floor. The windows were open, and neither the storm nor we slept that night. Our beginning was a surprise to both of us, and even more a surprise when it turned into years together. At the time, we were each other's rebound relationships, and we knew what everyone said about the shelf life of rebound lovers.

Maybe that first night together is why storms work like an aphrodisiacs for me. This night, the lightning and thunder breathing over our house, we found ourselves back in the quiet familiars of each other. Ken's hand moved across the scars, the stitches still in, the feeling along a wide band simply gone. Dead zone skin on my inner left arm, where the removal of lymph nodes a year ago took away some nerve endings. Now across my chest dead letters. Empty lots. The space between what feels. What to do with this numbness?

I told myself I was lucky, considering that some people don't even get to have sex lives, let alone spend 20 years with someone who was still attracted to them and committed to their marriage, yet still I felt like something was gone. For weeks after the surgery, I could feel something like a phantom nipple, but eventually that faded along with the phantom milk-dropping feeling. But now as the storm passed over, I found myself in the dark, naked in a way I had never been before with the man I loved.

Sex was something different now, an unnamed animal in the forest. So in the weeks after the surgery we touched slowly, tentatively, trying to learn this new language of the body that spoke of desire but also of loss, and spoke mostly in the diction of not-knowing.

Sex wasn't the only thing that happened during storms. There was a major event that spring that would be referenced for years to come whenever someone said, "Tornado. Lawrence." The storm was huge, and errant cells spouted large and unruly twisters. Ken, a devotee of all things weather-related, rushed into the bedroom where I was casually listening to Celtic music, oblivious that destruction was on its way.

"A tornado a half-mile wide is coming straight for our house. It's only about 20 miles to the southwest right now, and it should be here soon."

I looked up. The sky did have that greenish-gray cast to it that told us crazy things—like hail or tornados—might fall out of it.

"What do you want to save?" Ken asked me casually.

I looked around the bedroom and got up, not really too excited by it all. "Okay, well, I guess we need to get the pets downstairs."

"Natalie already has all her frogs in the basement, and she's getting the cats right now."

"Hmmm…okay, let's get the photo albums." After the photo albums, I gathered up little gifts I'd received from people over the last year or two: some precious stones, some earrings, some figurines of cows on parade, some sea shells. Then I walked through the house, looking at everything. I figured if the tornado sprawled our clothes all over the place, it wouldn't be such a big deal, because we could find what we could and take it all to a Laundromat. Or replace it. The furniture was used anyway, and it might be nice to get new stuff. I could give up the dishes, the records, the toys, the houseplants.

Ken looked at me. "Anything else worth saving?"

"I think I can just let the rest of it go."

We walked slowly downstairs, where Ken had a weather radio, a regular radio, and the computer on line, all giving us minute-by-minute updates. The tornado was slow-moving, and during the 15 or so minutes we waited for it to get to us, I wandered around the yard with Forest. At one point, we climbed the stairs to the deck and looked west toward the blackness at the edge of the sky.

"Well, I guess I'm just like a cat with nine lives," Forest said. His hair was buzzed off, and I loved petting his puppy head.

"What do you mean?"

"I died once in the accident and then came back, and now we have this tornado coming, and I'll live through that too."

I hugged him and we went into the basement, where Natalie was huddled on a sleeping bag in the very back corner, clutching the cat in a carrying case, watching frogs from three different tanks now mixed up together, but luckily not chomping on one another, and shaking. "It's going to be okay," I told her.

"No, it isn't," she said, in tears. She had her old pink Barbie blanket around her shoulders.

I reached and tried to hold her, but she pulled away, too afraid to let anyone see or touch her at the moment. I understood, so I backed away for now.

Meanwhile, there was a sound outside, almost like a faraway train, just like tornados were supposed to sound. In my 20 years of living in the Midwest, I had never seen a tornado, but I had wanted to do so desperately (from a safe distance, of course) all along. Now that one was coming, I didn't feel so much like I needed to see it, to experience it rumbling over my house, tearing it away, scattering my life.

Yet I felt strangely peaceful. I didn't doubt for a moment that we could survive tucked into the crawl space behind the basement, safely underground. At the same time, with all we had been through, a tornado would have been redundant.

In the end, the tornado lifted up, switched direction, thinned down to a skinny strand, and (from our vantage point, after we raced out of the basement, jumped into the van, and charged up the driveway to get a better view) brushed the southwestern part of town. "God's finger," Ken said to the kids, who, having watched too many Austin Powers movies, started joking, "A hundred million dollars!" and putting their pinkies to the edge of their lips, just like Dr. Evil did.

The tornado did several millions dollars' worth of damage, relatively minor for a tornado, especially for those of us who live in tornado alley and generally measured the severity of twisters by what couldn't be replaced. Luckily, this one didn't take anyone's life, although it did eat away at some apartment buildings and lift mailboxes out by their roots and toss them around.

Grief was a funny thing, kind of like the weather in Kansas or any place that changes suddenly and drastically. It was something uncharitable, yet totally tender.

About six months after the breast surgery, a sudden sadness caught me off-guard, ignited whenever Ken pulled my body close to him at night and started running his hands over me. I tried to do the normal things, react in the usual ways, but a part of me wasn't showing up to join the rest of me, not to mention the all of him.

One evening, I had to tell him.

"Look, I don't know how to say this, but I don't want to have sex anymore. At least not for a while."

He looked up from the book he was reading. We were sitting in our bedroom, him on the floor, leaning against the bed, and me in the easy chair, worn even more by now and not exactly reclining on cue any longer. He looked up, a tad curious, but there was nothing of anger or grief in his face.

"I mean," I said, wondering how he was going to take this, "I just don't feel like I'm there when we…"

"I noticed," he answered. How could he not?

"Maybe we just need to do it all slower, and not so late at night when the kids are over in the next room. Maybe I just need a transition time." A moratorium on sex, that's what I was asking for, and I didn't know for how long or why or how.

I felt my head swimming in its confused flood. I had always loved sex, considered it one of the great perks of being alive. Maybe it was all the trauma. Maybe it was all the loss. I couldn't tell who I was anymore, as if I had just fallen through what seemed like solid ground, and I was still in free fall.

"I don't know what you want to do, but…"

"I can handle it," he answered, smiling.

"It's really okay?"

"It's really okay."

Weeks later, we went to a retreat center together, getting away from our house, phone, email, kids, people dropping by, tasks that were never done, memories of all that had fallen away. The second afternoon we were there, in a small cabin in the deep woods, it rained. When we heard the water hitting the roof, eventually pounding through the trees to the ground, we looked up from the magazines we were reading. We looked at each other.

"You have no idea how scared I was," he said. I knew he wasn't talking about sex or the lack thereof. "I thought I was going to lose you."

I looked into his eyes, the blue turning greener over the years, shining brighter as his faced aged, his hair grayed. He looked back, the one who had held the lion's share of the anxiety, the fear, not to mention the weight of the laundry, too. The one who'd held me in the middle of the night, when I woke up trapped in a nightmare, or at mid-morning, my hand in his under the oncology center table as we reviewed statistics and protocols.

When I returned his gaze, it was like a thousand other times and yet I was also seeing him for the first time: this man with whom I had shared a bed, home, children, cancer, and many meals, and yet the familiar shape of him held something completely unknown to me too.

I wish I could say that at this moment my body ignited with passion and all was well and easy from that point on, but it was more like dipping my toes back into the water, startled at the temperature and softness, and then starting to move, relearning old ways of moving until I realized nothing was forgotten. It took time for memories of sex with breasts to recede, like a ship I once inhabited, a place that moved so far over the horizon it began to seem unreal that it ever actually existed.

My journey away from sex, because it wasn't what it used to be, and then back again to move through it as something new, yet familiar, would startle me periodically over the next few years. It was one of those things we didn't read much about in all the pastel pamphlets about living with cancer displayed in oncology and surgery offices, except for a sentence or two about decreased libido.

But for the moment, at least, I found my way back to Ken even though I felt enormous fear, deep grief around all the edges. I put down my magazine and rolled toward him. Sometimes you have to leave to come home. Sometimes you have to let in the hardest stuff to do the easiest. Love and Death, so goes the Woody Allen movie title. Two sides of the same glimmering coin, twirling on its way down.

Outside, there wasn't a thunderstorm, but there might well have been one.

Labyrinth

The labyrinth was in the woods, with a good view on clear days, if you could get past the trees, of Pike's Peak, not far from Colorado Springs. I was there with a group of a dozen women taking part in a six-day poetry therapy intensive in the tender month of June, the air refreshing and the light fine.

My first time walking the labyrinth came after eight hours of workshops and just before dinner. A woman I didn't know was already walking it, but I started anyway. It was a huge labyrinth, modeled after the famous one in Chartres, France, except that it was outdoors and built out of white rocks over a slope as curvy as the surface of the ocean. Trees occasionally lined the path or stood slightly to the side. The air was clean and dry, just beginning to chill.

I began following the path, stopping to touch each tree, feel its bark under my palm. My feet walked the path carefully, my mind repeating one chant or another. The air was potent with the scent of pine and fir. It took a long time, 20 minutes or more to reach the center, and there I found four stone benches in a circle, and in the middle, a small offering of branches and statues, feathers and rocks. On my way back out, I met the other woman. She bowed and smiled. I bowed and smiled back.

The next day, our whole group walked the labyrinth together, with instructions that afterwards, we were to write in our journals. I began again, and this time, whenever I met a tree, I leaned into it, held it close to my body as if it were a dearly-beloved friend. Whenever I met some of the women, we would hug each other this same way, no words, all presence.

At the center, in the hot sun, I reached into my pocket, found only a little square of chocolate which I fed into the offering. Then I started out, embracing trees and women all the way.

As I went, I realized something: when you walked out of a traditional labyrinth like this, it seemed that you were headed from the center of the center right out into the world again. Then the path turned abruptly, and you had 20 minutes or more of going in circles, back and forth, up and down. This was where I was in my healing from cancer and my father's death, too. I was finished with the surgeries, the chemo, the bulk of the lab tests and the waiting for results. It seemed I was done, but really, I had just left the center, and walking all the way out would take as long, if not longer, than walking in. I would also change in the process.

Yet I knew some things to sustain me. When I met a woman on the path, I hugged her. I did the same with anything else I encountered—trees, chemo, hard medicine, bad news, good news, children, friends, sorrow. Embrace, and then let go.

A few years later, back in Vermont for another Goddard College residency, I remembered the Colorado labyrinth as I entered the Haybarn, where Angela, a graduating student had arranged her own labyrinth, its edges dotted with candles in the dark, enormous room which doubled as an auditorium and large workshop space. Sitting around the edge, I could make out the lines and curves, going in and back out again. Angela had just written a memoir and study on pilgrimage, and the labyrinth encapsulated the same resonance of any journey that is largely guided by mystery and discovery as we take the next step, not knowing where we'll land.

When she called for volunteers to walk the labyrinth in the grayish-blue light of the Haybarn, I stood up and started toward the entrance. Life could pick us up—even if we were unwilling hitchhikers—for such trips every now and then, and you might as well jump eagerly in the vehicle and enjoy the scenery.

Crying Women

When Ken and I arrived at the oncology office, we saw a mother and daughter, straddling the near side and far side of middle age. Both of them wept. The mother looked especially stricken as she stood behind her daughter, one hand on her daughter's shoulder as the daughter handed the receptionist an insurance card to copy. Neither woman spoke.

We handed the receptionist our new insurance card, too, and then sat down, still scared just a little after several days of absolute terror sanded down slightly by the constant distractions of regular life. It had all started a few weeks ago with a pain in my right hip that wouldn't subside. I had decided it was from taking a long walk on Christmas day that involved hauling my out-of-shape body up a hill and back down again. Friends told me it was arthritis or muscle ache or anything else that didn't sound like bone cancer.

But just to be sure, I called Dr. Stein's office, certain they would suggest a few x-rays. When they called back to recommend a bone scan, the old robot from the TV series *Lost in Space* sprung to mind, waving its arms, rushing back and forth while yelling, "Danger, danger, Will Robinson!" But after checking my dreams, which didn't indicate danger, only the constant exploration of new houses and strange drives in old red trucks, and after dining with multiple friends who charmed me with lines like, "You're healthy as a horse," I calmed down. Somewhat.

This turned out to be just one of several kinds of scans and varieties of scares that were to come over the next year whenever something, like constant headaches or a pulled muscle in my shoulder, erupted. Each time, there would be the terror at the thought of that Russian roulette word— recurrence—and the intense relief when the call came that everything was okay.

The day of the bone scan, my first such one, I got injected with radioactive fluid that would magically light up any new growth in my bones once it made the fast tour of my body over the course of four hours. I went to a coffee house to work on my laptop, knowing I was radioactive but staying somewhat cheerful, due to the strength of the coffee and my own denial. When I returned for the scan, meeting Ken at the hospital this time, I found that I couldn't lie on the steel table with the steel humming plate over my head without panicking, so Ken held my hand and recounted the details of the sunset and the sand at Key West while the radiologist played beautiful music.

Finally, the machine hummed its way below my eyes, which had been closed tightly while I cajoled myself not to give in to the temptation to open them and freak out all over again. A screen suspended over me showed (at least to my eyes, separated from their eyeglasses) what seemed like long lines of my own bones and muscles. Finally the technician, a kind man, adjusted the screen and I realized the bones and muscles were actually rocks and running water that correlated to the dreamy piano and guitar music playing. I spent the rest of the scan staring intently at the idyllic nature scenes while this giant machine traveled over me, kind of like I was being felt up by an alien. I imagined Ursula with me, her calming presence, and took some deep breaths.

At home a few days later, the call came: nothing in my hip, it was completely clear, but there was something else, and it was in my head. It looked like the bone in my forehead was overly thick, which probably meant nothing but we would need more x-rays.

Brain tumor. Bone cancer. The phrases echoed through the halls of my fear, and I found myself weathering a good many fear storms only made worse when I realized Ken was experiencing the same weather. "It's just old stuff coming up, your old issues about cancer, maybe mine too," he told me when I asked him, for the hundredth time, if he was sure it was nothing.

Sometimes I felt so afraid I didn't know if I could do anything else. But I took the next breath, and the next, and eventually the fear would relax a little too, or perhaps I just got more numb. I wondered if I was so good at denial that I did in fact have a recurrence, but didn't know it because I had convinced my friends, my dreams even, that I was fine. I wondered if I could trust my own instincts.

Now it was the day of the appointment, and Ken and I sat in the oncology office again, me holding the heavy envelope of x-rays on my lap. Soon we would hear something. "I just want to be okay," I'd told·Nancy, right in the middle of the dairy section of the food co-op, "and get to that five year mark, where you are, so I can feel like I'm really clear of it."

"You're never really clear of it," she told me. My mother told me the same thing when I spoke with her.

But for now, on this January afternoon in the oncology office, they called the two crying women in, then us. I stood behind the women, the mother now weeping conspicuously while her daughter stepped onto the scale and tried to hold in the chaos and pain so she wouldn't weigh too much. Eventually they went to their room, and we went to ours.

When Dr. Stein came in, and whipped out old x-rays to compare to the new ones, the relief on his face was obvious.

"Oh, look at this. You've had this all along," he said, pointing to a place in the center of my forehead, just a little to the right, where my bones fused together in a slightly pointed way. "It's actually very common that things like this show up in bone scans." So I had a pointed head, a slightly-extraterrestrial-looking brain.

Ken and I looked alertly toward him, both of us exhaling.

"You mean I'm really okay? I've been freaking out for days."

"I really think you're fine, but I don't want to oversell this. Let's do another x-ray of your forehead, and then some blood work just to be sure."

After we made him repeat this several times, we focused on the normal parts of the check-up—the breastless exam, going over my list of little ailments so he could find out how the hiatal hernia was doing and speculate that my hip pain may have had something to do with wearing worn-out tennis shoes on long walks. We shook hands, joked about how I had a little antenna made of bone, and got the necessary paperwork for a blood test, head x-rays, and two new mastectomy bras.

On the way out, the two crying women were in front of us. The mother was no longer crying, but the daughter was weeping vigorously as she bid her doctor goodbye. Her slim shoulders shook as she clasped her hands over her stomach. Her pink face gleamed.

"I just can't believe it. This is so wonderful," she said.

"I knew you would be pleased, and isn't it such a relief?" asked her doctor, who nodded and smiled in his white hair and white lab coat.

They reached the front desk ahead of us, and the receptionist came around and gave the crying daughter a big hug. "I don't know why I'm crying so much," the daughter said.

"Oh, it's just fine," said the receptionist.

Ken and I looked at each other—two women in front of us had prepared themselves for a death sentence, and then, miraculously, found that was not what was happening at all. Obviously, the opposite outcome happened enough to make these moments shine like small, well-polished miracles. In the end, the statistics meant nothing. Either you were 100% alive or you were looking toward a future of leaving that 100% life behind, a future coming full force at you, in whatever form it was taking at the time, much sooner than you would have planned.

I was okay, but I also realized I had gained this new peripheral vision. Everything was lit from within in its unpredictability, in its magic too. Tears of pain and fear, and tears of joy and freedom—no difference between them at times.

The Body Erotic

When Rhonda, a student taking pictures of women of all shapes, naked and in natural light, asked me to pose, I told her yes, thinking it would be good for me. Besides, I wanted to contribute to putting out into the world images of bodies like mine, to place my own chest next to the wonder and power of images such as the famous poster of writer Deena Metzger stretching her arms to the sky in joy, naked, after her mastectomy. I was a little nervous about having myself displayed topless (and I mean really topless) alongside some of my students, so it took us six months to get around to setting up the photography session.

In the middle of a winter, fierce even for central Vermont, Rhonda and I went to an empty second-story room in one of the dorms. It was between workshops and dinner, and we acted like this was just a normally-scheduled event. The room had only an unused, made-up bed in it and a few chairs, plus a mini refrigerator where we faculty stored our booze and onion dip. It was the space where we all met each evening to complain and laugh. Now the room was just a quiet ghost, open to whatever visited it. The windows were full of clouds and snow, filling the room with gray light.

First, she photographed me with my clothes on. "Just look into the camera," she told me, half-climbing on a chair, balancing her elegant body despite the multiple sclerosis that made it hard for her to flow from one shape effortlessly into another. Her long straight hair fell to one side as she leaned over, bracing her boots on the chair.

I looked into the camera. I did not offer the slight smile that usually was painted across my face in photographs, the smile that I'd practiced before many mirrors over many years, the one that made me look mildly content but also hid my double chin just a little. Instead, I just looked, and I knew already that my eyes were sad.

Then I took off my sweater, my bra heavy with the prostheses. I stood by the door, and she backed herself against a corner on the other side of this small room. I lifted my arms to the ceiling and looked up. I knew this was not a beautiful sight in any of the ways I'd been taught to see beauty in a woman. I knew rather that it was beautiful in the way that a field is beautiful, even though some of its edges sheer off violently due to erosion. I knew it was the beauty of change and pain, the beauty of loss, the beauty of being beyond even loss in a place I cannot name.

How do I sing the body erotic?

I lifted my arms high and kept staring into the ceiling, knowing even now my eyes carried this pain. I put my arms down and looked straight into her camera. She snapped again, a cacophony of clicks, a beautiful rhythm of shutter.

She walked over to me and looked carefully at the scars.

"I've never seen a mastectomy before," she said, more out of curiosity than anything else. I let her look, remembering how she once told me she wanted children but probably wouldn't be able to have any because of the MS, because of what her disease might do to her pregnancy, or how pregnancy might worsen her disease, or because she never knew if she would have enough energy to get through the day. The worries we carry all the time under our clothes.

I sat on the side of the bed and she shot more photos. Soon she was climbing up on a shelf and leaning over, balancing herself as carefully as possible, saying it was hard to do this now, but she really wanted to get the best shot, saying that there was not really enough light but still enough, that she didn't really have the right lens but still the lens would work.

I looked deeply into the camera in a way I never had before. I leaned my arm on the windowpane and watched the dark circle of the small lens glass in the camera that saw me seeing it. I knew that, however this photo came out, it would really be me. I also knew that it would hurt to look at it, that I would have to find a way to see. More like the way to love the body long after it had ceased to look like anything close to what resembled youth

206

and beauty, at least not beauty apart from the aging of trees and motion of weather.

A few months later, I sat on the floor of my bedroom and pulled Rhonda's photos out of the thick, cardboard envelope. There were 21 shots of me on contact paper, first a row of me sitting with my clothes on, smiling, looking somewhat like I thought I looked (but why was my hair sticking up funny?). Then me, naked from the waist up, at first smiling, and then not so much. Holding the fake boobs in my hands, lifting my arms to the sky, touching my empty chest.

The shot that spoke to me the most, though, was one I didn't remember Rhonda taking. I was standing, my hands barely touching over my stomach. My head was tilted just a bit to one side. I looked scared, calm, happy, sad, steady, relieved. The things I didn't like about my appearance were there— the dark circles about my eyes, my lack of a firmly-defined chin, the hair that has its own agenda, and the extra weight. The pockets of fat at my sides were caught in the spotlight after years of being upstaged by the star power of the breasts. I could see the faint scars across my chests, the spot where the chemo port went in and out, and the whiteness of my skin.

All my life, I had fretted about my body in the same boring and usual way as just about every other woman I'd ever known, and that old hatred and worry filled the background of each photo. Yet in the center of each, there was just me, a 44-year-old woman with some of her trails and trials more visible than others. It wasn't what I would call sexy or beautiful, yet it was alive. Erotic, I supposed, if I were brave enough to claim that word.

I smiled, not one of those camera-facing-me smiles, and told my dubious thoughts to just hang tight with such a statement. Breastless. Erotic. I tried to stop myself from adding "anyway" or "regardless," tried to accept that this body, shaped by so many years of food, activity, sleep, and thought, and then cut, healed over, and scarred, was still the place where I live.

I took a breath, slowly, and put the contact sheet back in the envelope. Outside, the cottonwood tree moved its leaves tentatively in the light wind. The sun was out, and soon, so was I, leaning on the railing of the deck to watch the wide horizon fill with a billowing thunderhead. No way of knowing yet if it would come together enough for another summer storm, or break apart. No way of knowing that a year from now, Rhonda would write me that, despite the impossibility of it all, she was pregnant, and later, she would send me emails in between chasing a toddler around in her wheelchair.

I watched and breathed in this body that was so much more aware of how anything can happen. In that awareness, there was so much room to get lost, and also so much to find. The sunlight lit the clouds from behind while a lightning bolt dropped down far away. The sky so large, and I knew how much I loved the sky.

Getting Found

It was exactly a year after the double mastectomy, a shadowy and damp Earth Day, which this year also doubled as career day for all the ninth-graders in our community. I had a slim, 14-year-old girl hanging out with me in coffee shops, me working on this memoir while she wrote fantasy stories about powerful women finding ways to persevere at the end of time. We occasionally walked the main downtown street, looking in windows, talking about the *Lord of the Rings* cast as she flipped her hair out of her eyes, and eventually settling down for spicy Thai soup that steamed up both our glasses. She was planning to become a scientist who wrote fantasy novels on the side.

When we returned to the coffee shop to write for another stretch, Daniel called me. His career day with a biologist had begun at 5 a.m. when they went 100 miles south to spy the booming prairie chickens. Now he was with another biologist, Stan, an older man with a cigar in his mouth who snapped his worn pickup truck around a nature preserve, reminiscing to Daniel about what kind of student Ken had been 30 years earlier. They were 20 miles or so north of town, doing pond repair, Daniel engrossed in the valiant rescue of pollywogs. He hadn't eaten all day, and he needed a ride. Now.

I bid farewell to my time-traveling companion and headed off with the scant directions Stan gave me, beginning with sentences like, "I don't know the name of that road, but it's where that school is—what is it called?—that they closed, and then you go a way until you see a beaten-up mailbox...."

Of course, I got lost cavorting up and down damp roads of packed-down mud and many-sized rocks. The sky was all around me, carrying a panorama of dramatic clouds that had just finished raining and were not quite sure they were ready to clear out, like a gang of drunken people in a bar who didn't yet know it was closing time.

I drove past an old house with a new mailbox, then past a triple-mailbox surrounded by newspaper boxes, and eventually past a mailbox painted like the American flag but with tiny crosses instead of stars, and surely not fifty of them. I pulled into a driveway and turned around, heading back over my tracks.

Driving that day was a lot like walking the labyrinth last spring, the way ahead seemingly leading out, but instead leading me back in and around. I told myself to just relax, sooner or later I would find the right beaten-up mailbox and follow it to my first-born. Soon I would aim the car back around to where I started, and find the entrance to the drive, just hidden by a few errant Osage Orange trees, the brain-like hedge apples scattered on the drive.

Now I let myself breathe slowly, the blue of the sky starting to bleed through the baring limbs of trees. Lost or found, I put my foot on the gas and unrolled the windows to let in more of the sky.

Epilogue: Happy Anniversary, Darling!

Anniversaries are major deals for survivors, and often the way we introduce ourselves to doctors, support groups, and other survivors: "Hello, my name is Caryn, and I'm a six-year survivor." It seems like something that would fit well on a stick-on name tag, yet it carries the weight of healing and defiance, hope and fear, the future and the past. At the same time, the word "anniversary" takes me back to Ricky and Lucy Ricardo in their black and white twin beds, calling out "Happy Anniversary, Darling" right before sleep and after one of Lucy's many mishaps, writ large across the television set of my childhood.

Still, I cling to my anniversary date, March 21st, the spring Equinox, as another fence post I've reached in my life's wandering through the wide prairie lands—no path often present—of struggles and arrivals. Since my cancer treatment ended, two conflicting impulses have been released into my bloodstream: to hold tight to the wider view of life that cancer gave me, and to get as much done as possible, because who knows when I'll die.

Let's just say that, at first, the "get as much done as possible" gene was dominant, which isn't so surprising given my history of packing my schedule to fill each pocket with something to do, my workaholic father, and my infatuation with starting new projects. I shot out of the cannon at high speed, adding to my life more administrative work related to my teaching job, and more writing projects, workshops, groups, and volunteer obligations.

But just like the earlier rise and fall from the chemo steroids, after flowing with this jet-stream for a while, I crashed into the ground, where I found my second impulse taking deeper root.

First Anniversary

Shortly after my final surgery, I get sick. Not very sick, more like vague flu-like symptoms, low-grade and persistent. At first, I think it's simply a virus, something impermanent, but after a few months, I begin to notice that I don't seem to ever get over it.

I take antibiotics, several times, and when none of those rounds make a difference, I try acupuncture, herbal tea, visits with Dr. Stein, visits with my general physician, and forays onto the internet. Over the next year, I get sick more often. Sinus pressure, drainage, slight fatigue, and bad headaches. It gets to the point that I start marking my calendar, keeping track, trying to find clues.

In my sessions with Ursula, I no longer see colors or hear birds singing, but sink into a quiet, deep gray, a comforting but sad place. Although I feel better after each time I lie on her table and feel the wind above me shift and my energy return a little more, I still yearn for the strength to clear the fence of this illness.

At the end of a year, I realize that I've been sick at least half the time, and while the illness isn't solid or forceful enough to keep me in bed too often, it does linger over me as I work, pick up kids, go out for Mexican food with Ken. A naughty companion that makes me miserable. A reason to carry around Excedrin and antihistamines, to search the food co-op regularly for some new remedy to try.

Nothing works.

"When will I get well?" I ask my friend Denise over the giant spring roll salad we share at a downtown restaurant.

"I don't know," she says, sympathetically. I try to laugh it off, take more pain-killers, drink more juice, hope for the best.

"I think I'll just call it 'the thing' because it's not allergy, virus, or anything else I can name," I tell her, and Dr. Stein. He believes it's environmental, or a cumulative effect of chemo, two directions I can't chart easily because of a lack of substantial research on what poisoning the body or poisoning the earth does to some of us. As someone who always caught viruses and developed headaches easily, I feel a little like the canary in the mine, inhaling deeply in hopes of some clean air.

My anniversary night falls on the meeting date of a transformative language arts writing group I lead for people living with cancer. I look at the square table surrounded by seven faces, and remember that the group last year had 12. Gone is an elegant retired nurse and lover of piloting planes, who came last spring wearing beautiful pink sweaters and accented scarves, saving her energy all day from her breast-to-liver metastasized cancer for a chance to write stories about her life. Gone is the young mother of two small boys who had been told she was probably going to be okay only to find, probably during the last days of her life, that she had a particularly aggressive kind of cancer that moved at lightning speed all through her organs. Gone is the woman who gave other members tremendously wry and wise support while she was caught in extensive treatment for rectal cancer. "I'm just a pain in the ass," she reminded us, months before her death.

In all these groups, at some point, someone brings up the proverbial hit-by-a-bus explanation of life's uncertainty. "I said that I had cancer," a man or woman in my group will say, "and my friend replied, 'Well, I could die tomorrow if I was hit by a bus.'" Everyone in the group laughs or groans, talks about how much they hate that bus metaphor. "Yeah, you could get hit by a bus, but right now you're fine, and I have cancer."

We spend a lot of time in these groups laughing and crying, probably about as much time as we do writing. Often, just introducing ourselves brings tears of relief—here, people can write about whatever they want without having to protect loved ones—and tears of fear and exhaustion from living on a moving walkway. Those tears also come from the caregivers, who feel that monumental pressure to hold up the other, to put their fear and dread on a shelf so they can get in the kitchen and cook up something good to eat, feed the life that feeds them.

But it's the laughter that stays with me—the jokes about "You look great!" and the comebacks of, "What do you mean? That I usually look like shit?" The way Lily begins one of her poems with, "Don't give me that look, that look that says I have Rumsey Funeral Home on speed dial." The cracks about how sexy we look without boobs or hair, with parts of a finger missing and thick ropey scars on our arms, wearing compression sleeves or carrying our canes.

When I get home one summer night, Ken asks, "Doesn't it hit on all your own cancer issues to do this work?" He thinks it might depress me, but no, it does the opposite.

I think of Linda, a writer and photographer who has been taking my Kansas City workshop throughout her late-stage ovarian cancer. Last week, Sue said to her, "You know, my breast cancer was caught early, and it's nothing compared to what you have. When I'm with you, I feel like I'm really okay."

"I'm glad my dying makes you feel better," Linda said with a straight face, her page boy wig distinguished, as she catapulted us all into the kind of laughter that takes your breath away. Sue almost fell out of her chair, and I was laughing so hard that I started crying.

Maybe my ease has to do with how Linda's dying helps me cultivate perspective, give up sweating the small stuff so much. But I suspect it has more to do with the courage I witness, week after week, in all the workshops

I do: the way that people are willing to take great risks in the stories they write and tell; how the veneer of what we think keeps us safe is gone in such workshops. What really matters is unearthing meaning, clearing the obstacles out of the way, including fear and doubt, insecurity and low confidence, to feel more alive in the process of creation.

It also has something to do with the stories I hear and the stories I witness. The man reads a poem he wrote to his wife, who just finished breast cancer treatment, about how strong she is, crying throughout his reading while reminding us, "Hey, I'm an engineer! I never cry, and in this workshop, I can't stop."

The way Julie, a mother of a four-year-old who's been through the breast cancer maze extraordinaire, calls herself the recovering Edgar Allen Poe of the group because she often writes about just how much cancer sucks.

I remember Linda's words, "I don't believe we were writing toward specific endings. They just happened serendipitously and wonderfully." She reads me one of her favorite endings, "Every fiber of me begs to wake up—to wake up, electric, stunned, and newly alive."

It's everything Linda says, that new life available at any given moment for the looking. The faint breeze that comes through us as we get ready to leave one place and land in another. All the time.

At the same time, I realize that who gets to live through cancer has nothing to do with personal goodness. I see women who have similar diagnoses to mine face recurrence or sudden death. While treatment choices, lifestyle, diet and attitude certainly weigh in on mortality, cancer is also so catalyzed by a complex web of what we know and what's beyond our knowing. A roll of the dice as to why Marla survives stage four breast cancer for five years, and why Edie endures three recurrences of what was supposed to be caught early and easy to treat. So often cancer has nothing to do with character, fairness, risk or daring.

Given the poisons infused in the soil, water and air, in our bodies and the bodies, stems, trunks and cores of other species, all I know is how much humans are not exempt from the earth. Some of us have a little more of the canary in the mineshaft in us than others, but we're all in the coal-mine together.

Second Anniversary

Mortality ripples through my family. After my discovery of harboring BRCA 1, my siblings are tested, and two out of three end up having the mutation docked at their station also. In the fall, Lauren goes through a long surgery to remove her breasts, uterus, cervix, and ovaries, leaving long lines of stitches which grow into scars. She also opts for slim breast inflators. After four very painful months of having saline solution inserted into those inflators until her breasts were pumped to size, the inflators are swapped out for silicon impacts.

"Gummy bear silicon," she tells me on the phone, trying to alleviate my fears, "so if they tear, they don't leak." She says lying on her stomach is just fucking weird, like having Barbie doll parts attached to her. "It's like lying on silicon breast implants," she says.

"What's that like?"

"I don't know," she says. "It just is what it is."

Next my mother discovers she has breast cancer again. "Enough!" she tells her doctor, requesting a double mastectomy. The surgery goes well and within a few weeks I am emailing her the names of a good prosthesis. A few months later, she has a notion that she should have a colonoscopy, although she isn't due for one. "I just thought that with all the cancer, I should do this," she tells me over the phone while sharing the news that she has colon cancer.

Her colon cancer is discovered early enough to leave her with the crazy choice of heavy-duty infused chemotherapy, a clinical trial that means she will receive either something that might work or a placebo, a chemo pill ("chemo-lite," we call it), or nothing. She submits her life to six months on the chemo pill, its symptoms, like most chemo treatments, snowballing over time, leaving her too tired to do more than sleep, eat, and sit on the couch. But that's over now, and she's back to a life dotted with doctor appointments and tests just to make sure no other cancer erupts.

After a family dinner in New Jersey that spring with my sisters and brother as well as my aunt there, the women in my family converge in the living room for dessert and passing our breasts around. "Look at this one, Ma. It's light, and it droops when I bend over. It's a great fake boob," I tell my mother. My aunt says she hates her prosthesis because it pulls on her scars. Lauren simply looks both ways to make sure the men folk are tucked into the back room to watch a baseball game before she flashes us.

"Well, you'll never need to wear a bra again," I tell her, looking at the perfectly round, symmetrical Barbie doll boobs.

"Yeah, and now all I need to do is pick out a skin color for the nipples."

"You pick out the color?" I asked as my aunt laughs, and my mother passes around a small bowl of dark chocolate. We all know already that it helps prevent cancer.

Five incidences of cancer, just between my mother and aunt. Two occurrences of pancreatic cancer, one each for my father and uncle, who both died in their early 60s. Counting cancers doesn't make sense to me, nor does seeing cancer as something peculiar to my family. All around, the stories add up to a larger story of how our poisoned air, water, and land eventually filters through us. Everything we do to this earth coming back full-circle.

"What would it take to really address cancer?" I ask Dr. Stein on the day of my second anniversary, my legs swinging from the examining table, and my backless gown hovering over me as he lifts it to look at my chest.

He puts down his stethoscope. "What it would take is too extensive for any of the powers that be to ever take on."

He and I have talked increasingly about the environmental factors, now better documented through studies such as a seven-year project jointly funded by the National Institute of Environmental Health Sciences and the National Cancer Institute on how environmental exposures predispose some women to breast cancer.

Cancer's environmental roots, the same ones that branch through my family and so many other families, are deeply tangled with the underlying economic roots of everything around us—energy, housing, production, even genetically-engineered seeds. To pull out even one solution is like trying to pull out a weed with roots through the roots of every other plant.

Third Anniversary

On a slightly cool March morning, we wake early to catch the plane to Mexico, where we will see Angelica, Laura, and others we bonded with at the bioregional congress over three years ago. Our trip also covers my third anniversary of being diagnosed, putting me only two years away from that mythic five-year mark when, if there's no problem, I'll be declared cured (as if anyone can truly be cured of swimming with stingrays and other fast-moving critters of mortality). Then again, it's not like I would want to be cured of knowing how human I am, or how fragile and sinewy and imaginative life is.

The actual day of the anniversary, I'm giving a transformative language arts writing workshop in Spanish at the Instituto Culturo de los Artes in Cuernavaca. Never mind that I don't speak Spanish; I have two lovely writers from the area, one on each side of me, to whisper stereo translations of what the 40 participants say and write.

"She sees herself as a chair, her family as a table," Kenia, a beautiful poet with a cherub face and red stilettos, says to me as an older woman with long, graying braids and red lipstick reads slowly. "The birds return, and the oceans swell with life," translates Elaina, a social worker who loves writing, while a young woman wearing a polished face and shimmering black dress leans forward, her elegant legs crossed, to read more.

Never mind, either, that this center, with interior and exterior balconies of white stone that promise romance, was once a hospital. Today, there are musicians, dancers, artists, and writers filling the brick plaza with fountains in its center, the balconies too.

"This place was once a terrible hospital where I almost died," Laura tells me as we walked there earlier. She was in a deadly car accident 20 years ago in which she lost all her teeth and broke her ribs and hips. At the time, this hospital was notorious for letting patients die so that the staff could sell their patients' vital organs for a hefty profit.

Now the room is full of poetry, my comments in English and their writing in Spanish translating continuously, filling the room with small invisible birds of rhythm and cadence.

We go on to the next exercise, drawing on Fabio Morabito's poem entitled, "No he amado bastante" which says, in English:

> I've never been in love enough
> with anything
> to realize that it takes
> assiduous lingering,
> not snatching things up on the wing.

People write about never having been in love enough with their mothers, their hunger for meaning, their losses, their visions, their husbands, their children, and especially, their bodies. I listen, two channels of language playing simultaneously, and I put my hand over my heart.

Fourth Anniversary

The hotel room is on the eighth floor, and, although it's a swanky place, the rooms are unduly small and there's a building, nondescript brick and dark at night, facing my windows. I'm in Boston at a conference, and I've been sicker more often than usual lately.

Just last week, at home during the fourth anniversary of the diagnosis, I slipped into a mentally-unstable place where all my symptoms merged: insomnia, headaches, terrible gastric pressure that made me occasionally throw up when I tried to swallow, the persistent flu-like symptoms. The sleep deprivation especially made me so scared that I couldn't stop crying. After pacing back and forth, agitating and thrashing against what I should do, Ken finally put the lounge chair cushion in the woods, and had me lie there with a blanket and branch until I calmed down. I let the wind and ground hold me until I slept.

My panic is fueled by not knowing what's wrong with me. Blood tests and various doctors have found nothing wrong with my immune system or sinuses. A chiropractor tells me I have millions of tiny bacterial infections from surgery, but that doesn't sound real to me either. The acupuncturist says it's my spleen. Ursula tells me she doesn't know what it is, but that I will find out eventually.

Now I'm in this hotel, it is cold out for early April, and I'm miserable. It doesn't help that I'm so busy, driving myself hard. In fact, I'm only here, despite my strong impulse to cancel this trip, because I'm executive director of this organization, inhabiting a volunteer position that funnels frustrating phone calls and floods of emails to me on a continual basis.

There is a lot to worry about, including whether I can get myself to sleep tonight, and how I'll cover all my commitments. I think about this as I stare at the building outside my window, straining to see the sky. The chair I'm in is comfortable, the bed is luxurious. Yet I'm not at all home here, so far from the ground, so blocked from the sky. I get up from the chair, try the television, find nothing all that exciting on its 57 channels, shut it off, and then drink a glass of water. I'm shaking a little. I haven't slept well in several nights and hardly at all last night. Reality is beginning to seem like a concept rather than reality. I'm afraid and hurting. The migraine is crushing, and my throat is sore.

I sit on the edge of the bed, terrified to go downstairs and see people who see me as the one who does it all. I only know that I have to leave the room, take the elevator down, and get outside where I can walk, breathe, find the sky again.

But before I do that, I hear one clear message, so obvious after months of spending so much time and money on healers, remedies, doctors and wishes: *If you want to heal your life, you have to change your life.*

The words land in me, and keep landing. That night, I resign from the organization. Then I start making calls, stepping down from boards and extra jobs, giving up various small tributaries of freelance income and community applause. It's easier than I thought. "Sorry, I can't present at your conference after all because I'm having health issues," I say. Everyone understands, since almost everyone I speak with is my age, overwhelmed, and trying to stay healthy.

The changes don't happen in a weekend, but gradually, over the next few years. I join a gym and make it a priority to go four or so times a week. I learn the cello. I say no to baking cookies for the school dance, and facilitating a meeting for a group getting started. I train other people to run some of my workshop series. I still find myself agonizing over how to spend my time, and then berating myself when I do too much and need to return home to sleep at mid-day, affected again by "the thing."

A few weeks later, Dr. Stein holds the latest test results that show me as healthy, normal in all areas. We've already tried some unconventional things, even a low dose of estrogen in case these boringly-mysterious symptoms are triggered by the drastic hormone changes cancer put me through. We tried x-rays and blood tests, and he even had me send him a long email detailing every nuance of my suffering.

He leans back in his chair. "Like I've told you before, we don't really know the long-term effects of treating cancer this way. Remember, we put your body through the wringer, young lady. It could be from the chemo."

I'm thinking the same thing, and I wonder what it will take for my body to find its way out of these woods where I'm lost for a year, for two years, for three years and counting. Or will this damage linger, easing up so minutely that it's hard to even recognize?

All I know is that to heal my life, I need to change my life.

Fifth Anniversary

The fifth anniversary is supposed to be the biggie, like the fiftieth anniversary of a marriage, something to celebrate with balloons and ballrooms, only for cancer, it's a quieter affair. We go to a place full of drama and herds of people from around the world: the Grand Canyon.

That afternoon, I walk down the path with Ken and Forest, the other kids back in the motel room fighting over the remote control. After colder temperatures than I expected for late March, the sun is back out, and it's nearing 50 degrees. Forest and I walk hand-in-hand around the path smoothed by millions of people over the years, encircling the interior of a large curve of rock.

We come to an arch of stone, and we take each other's picture there, standing in that protected place of light and stone, dirt and depth. When I look down, even after walking for an hour, I still can't see the bottom, only clusters of green treetops, more slants and half-circles of reddening stone. I wonder what it's like down there, but for now, there's only the walk back up, and the need to lean against the canyon wall as the long line of tourist-laden donkeys passes by.

The next day, we leave early to visit friends in Santa Fe, encouraging the kids to wrap themselves up in fleece in their car seats and return to sleep. It's just barely light, and driving east from the canyon, we soon have to turn on our windshield wipers to clear the snow, falling sparsely at first, and then fierce and full, the flakes large as quarters.

Over the next three hours, we drive through multiple nuances of winter and spring, the light hidden, the light returning. Crossing the Navajo reservation, which holds the Hopi reservation, which holds more of the Navajo reservation, we change time zones seven times.

Time and weather. Ken's hands steady on the wheel, his eyes take in the rises and falls of land, the way a small cottonwood on a hill leans north from the south wind, the details of a kind of sage he remembers from years before, and at the same time, the road.

About a year after my treatment ended, I began co-writing songs with rhythm and blues singer Kelley Hunt. Our first song—which we were brought together to write for a breast cancer awareness show featuring her songs, my poetry, and a dance troupe—is one of my favorites, especially the bridge of the song: "I love this body that's not the way I thought. I love these people who help me through the dark. I love this life that keeps me waking up."

I hear Kelley singing those words in my mind now as I watch the sky, how it deepens just a little around the edges of mountains, trees, clouds. Her voice is deep and wide, a little like a river rushing through a narrow pass of ancient rock. I lean back and listen. Our fiercest losses can bring us closer to each other and the earth. Every place we go just another way to step into the air, to land on the ground.

Sixth Anniversary

The sixth anniversary passes unnamed, but I remember it as I wait for my chicken enchiladas somewhere in the middle of Ohio with Ken, Forest, and Natalie. Daniel is at college, a small Mennonite school in Newton, Kansas, where he can study environmental science, find that everyone in the 550-member student body is a friend, and hold down two jobs, vacuuming the cafeteria and weeding a small native prairie. We're on our way back from New Jersey, where we just helped my mother move Henry into a Jewish nursing home where they do wheelchair T'ai Chi to old Yiddish folksongs. His chemo treatments for pancreatic cancer have shrunk his tumor but also sparked a kind of trauma-induced dementia. A rare effect, we're told.

The trip is sudden. My mother called to give me an update on Henry, and since spring break was upon us, I hung up, and called Ken to see if he could take off work for a week, and we started driving. Now, five days later, we're driving west.

Again, it's the spring equinox, March 21st, the same day I was told I had cancer. The anniversary passes me as I pass it. "How long has it been?" a friend with lung cancer will ask me a month from now, and I'll tell her my last anniversary. In the uncontrolled cellular sprawl of this disease, so much gets measured by either fruit (as in, "his tumor was the size of a grapefruit") or anniversaries. As if a seasonal marker is a kind of victory.

"You're still here," I tell Linda in the writing group after she recounts her death sentence, two to five years according to an oncologist six years ago.

"Yes, I am," she answers, then opens her book to begin writing.

A year from now, a month from now, a day from now: a game I play with myself to try to grasp what's ungraspable. Time moves like water. Change is life. Even in stillness, motion.

An hour from now, I will be carrying a suitcase, computer, bag of oranges, pillow, and large bag of toiletries across a parking lot. It will be dark, the sky moist with the rain about to break, the wind slightly balmy, slightly chilled as it pours across me. I will struggle to balance everything, and at that moment I'll tell myself: see the beautiful world as it's happening.

But for now, I'm placing a small piece of these delicious chicken enchiladas on Ken's plate, asking Natalie how she likes her salad, and helping Forest remove the extra cheese from his tacos. I lift my water glass, take a sip. Water. Time. Change.

I tell my body, this body which is my most local address on the earth, "Happy Anniversary, Darling."

Acknowledgments

This is a true story, and true people have given me strength and comfort throughout every aspect of it, no one more than my husband, Ken Lassman, who held me together, body and soul, night and day, with our three children, Daniel, Natalie and Forest. I'm also indebted to Ursula Gilkeson, my friend and energy healer who brought love and light to chemo appointments, surgeries, and the spaces in between. As well, I'm forever grateful to Judy Roitman, who was with me, by phone or in person, almost daily. Special thanks to Jerry Sipe for being utterly present, truly a Kansas Bodhisattva who showed me how to simply be. Thank you with all my heart to my very wise and compassionate oncologist, Dr. Matt Stein, and my surgeons, Dr. Amie Jew, Dr. Brenda Lofton, and Dr. Julia Chapman.

This story would not be in your hands if not for the dedicated work of my publisher, Steve Semken, who believes in the power of words to help us better understand and connect with the world in which we live. Ice Cube Press is an important source for heartland writers.

There are a multitude of other people, friends and family, important to this story as it unfolded: particularly my mother and stepfather, Barbara Goldberg and the late Henry Newman, whose voices kept me afloat throughout my story; my siblings Lauren Pacheco, Jennifer Applequist, and Barry Goldberg; my in-laws, Alice Lassman and the late Gene Lassman; my healing group, Nancy O'Connor, Jim Lewis, Laurie Ward (who also served as my cancer press secretary), Diane Silver, Joy DeMaranville, Jo Andersen, Denise Low, Susan Elkins, and Jack Winerock; Anna Holcombe for taking such good care of our kids and house throughout much of this; and many dear friends and family far and near: Jeannette Shawl, Victoria Sherry, Margo MacLeod, Suzanne Richman, Sara Norton, Joseph Gainza, Francis Charet, Karen Campbell, Barb Dineen, Kelly Barth, Dixie Lubin, Courtney Skeeba, Denise Whitesides-Skeeba, Jordana Arnold, Linda

Lassman, Karen Lassman-Eul, Sandy Brungardt, Rita de Quercus, Laura Kuri, Angelica Flores, Paul Caviness, the late Weedle Caviness, and many others. I'm also grateful to friends who regularly sent prayers and wishes from the Lawrence Jewish Community Center, the Continental Bioregional Congress, Goddard College (and especially my students in Transformative Language Arts), the Franklin-Douglas Counties Coalition of Concerned Citizens (aka the Highway 59 group), the Kansas Area Watershed Council, and the National Association for Poetry Therapy.

I'm thrilled to have had so much support from dear writer friends while I wrote this book. Thanks to Katie Towler, Denise Low, Victoria Sherry, Nancy Hubble, Analisa Lee, Marianela Medrona-Marra, Kelley Hunt, Harriet Lerner, and all the women of the Wabi-Sabi Club. Thanks to the places where I composed much of this book: Milton's, Z's Divine Espresso, Mirth, Aimee's Coffeehouse, Signs of Life, and Henry's. Please note that some names throughout this book have been changed to protect people's privacy.

I can only wish that anyone going through cancer has this kind of healing community. It's one of the greatest things we can give to and receive from each other.

Related Organizations & Institutions

—**Continental Bioregional Congress**: Bioregionalism is a comprehensive "new" way of defining and understanding the place where we live, and living in that place sustainably and respectfully. What bioregionalism represents, identification with place and its history and culture, and living within the laws of nature, is new only for people who come out of the Western industrial-technological heritage. The essence of bioregionalism has been reality and common sense for native people living close to the land for thousands of years, and remains so for human beings today. At the same time, bioregional concepts are rigorously defensible in terms of science, technology, economics, politics, and other fields of "civilized" human endeavor. Bioregionalists are lifelong students of how to live in balance with our eco-communities. We recognize that we are part of the web of the life, and that all justice, freedom and peace must be grounded in this recognition. Bioregionalism re-connects us into the living biosphere through the Places where we live. By discovering our connections to the planet, we find a context for our lives to grow in. This context allows us to find ways to live sustainably in our settlements while at the same time provides us ways to nurture and restore the more-than-human community that surrounds us and which we are dependent on in so many ways. For more information, please see www.bioregional-congress.org.

—**Kansas Area Watershed Council**: KAW Council is one of the oldest bioregional organizations on the continent, founded in 1982. Explore and celebrate the prairie ecosystem, particularly in the Kansas Area Watershed, which encompasses much of Kansas, some of Nebraska and Colorado. Learn more about the kinds of events and gatherings we hosted, and the presentations we sponsored over the years. Please join us at our regular meetings, workshops, potlucks, and campouts to knit together community and sense of place, and to explore how to live in balance with the prairie ecosystem. Many of us are active in continental bioregional organizing, local peace and justice work, ecofeminism, wetlands preservation, prairie restoration, holistic health and healing, consensus training, and many manner of enhancing and sustaining local culture. www.kawcouncil.org, www.kawcouncil.blogspot.com

—**Goddard College**: Goddard is a small college in rural Vermont for plain living and hard thinking. Founded in 1863, Goddard is recognized for innovation in education. Its mission is to advance the theory and practice of learning by undertaking new experiments based upon the ideals of democracy and the principles of progressive education asserted by John Dewey. Goddard students are regarded as unique individuals who will take charge of their learning and collaborate with other students, staff, and faculty to build a strong community. Goddard encourages students to become creative, passionate, lifelong learners, working and living with an earnest concern for others and the welfare of the Earth. www.goddard.edu

—**Transformative Language Arts**: Transformative Language Arts is a new and emerging academic field focused on social and personal transformation through the power of the written, spoken or sung word. Drawing on all of the language arts, Transformative Language artists bring the language arts to community-building, cultural and ecological restoration, personal development, and many other areas of individual and collective liberation. Transformative Language artists, scholars, facilitators, and consultants facilitate creativity and language arts in many venues, such as community centers, schools, prisons, health centers and hospitals, businesses, research facilities, retreat centers, and more, facilitating creativity and language arts. TLA was founded in 2000 by Caryn Mirriam-Goldberg with a lot of help from faculty and students. Please see www.goddard.edu. For more information on TLA, also see www.TLANetwork.org and web.goddard.edu/~tla

CARYN MIRRIAM-GOLDBERG is the Poet Laureate of Kansas, and a long-time bioregionalist, poet and writer. She is the author of four collections of poetry, *Animals in the House* (Woodley Memorial Press), *Lot's Wife* (Woodley Memorial Press), *Landed* (Mammoth Publications) and *Reading the Body* (Mammoth Publications); an award-winning writing book, *Write Where You Are* (Free Spirit Press); and the editor of *The Power of Words: A Transformative Language Arts Reader*. She founded and coordinates Transformative Language Arts at Goddard College, where she teaches, and she facilitates writing workshops, particularly for people living with serious illness. With rhythm and blues singer-songwriter Kelley Hunt, she also performs and leads Brave Voice writing and singing workshops and retreats. Caryn helped found the Kansas Area Watershed Council, the Continental Bioregional Congress, and the Transformative Language Arts Network. She makes her home with her family just south of Lawrence, Kansas, in the Wakarusa river valley. FMI: www.CarynMirriamGoldberg.com

JOAN FOTH (cover art) is a native of New York and then a resident of Kansas and New Mexico, noted for her panoramic watercolor landscapes. She graduated from the High School of Music and Art in New York City and earned a degree in Art History and Oriental Studies at Barnard College. Her successful career began in Kansas, where she lived with her husband. In 1970, she was one of the first recipients of an artist-in-residence grant from the National Endowment for the Arts along with many other awards and fellowships. Her art has appeared at galleries throughout the country, and on the cover of *Prairyerth* by William Least Heat Moon.

The Ice Cube Press began publishing in 1993 to focus on how to best live with the natural world and to better understand how people can best live together in the communities they inhabit. Since this time, we've been recognized by a number of well-known writers, including Gary Snyder, Gene Logsdon, Wes Jackson, Patricia Hampl, Micheal Pollan, Jim Harrison, Annie Dillard, Kathleen Norris, Janisse Ray, Alison Deming and Barry Lopez. We've published a number of well-known authors as well, including Mary Swander, Jim Heynen, Mary Pipher, Bill Holm, Carol Bly, Marvin Bell, Debra Marquart, Ted Kooser, Stephanie Mills, John T. Price, Bill McKibben and Paul Gruchow. Check out our books at our web site, with booksellers, or at museum shops, then discover why we are dedicated to "hearing the other side."

Ice Cube Books
205 N Front Street
North Liberty, Iowa 52317-9302
steve@icecubepress.com
www.icecubepress.com

surprise surprise ... to the higher than the sky gang
Laura Lee & Fenna Marie

PAPERBINDER

02/10

orce.